The Brat Pack

The Brat Pack

ELEVEN TO FOURTEEN YEAR OLDS
HOW DO YOU TREAT YOURS?

John and Sue Ritter

Marshall Pickering
An Imprint of HarperCollins*Publishers*

Marshall Pickering is an imprint of
HarperCollins*Religious*
Part of HarperCollins*Publishers*
77–85 Fulham Palace Road, London W6 8JB

First published in Great Britain
in 1994 by Marshall Pickering

10 9 8 7 6 5 4 3 2 1

John and Sue Ritter assert the moral right to
be identified as the authors of this work

A catalogue record for this book is
available from the British Library

ISBN 0551 02757-6

Printed in Great Britain by
HarperCollinsManufacturing Glasgow

Contents

Acknowledgements

Thanks:
To the kids of MARSHLAND SCHOOL in West Walton, Cambs. They feature on the front cover and were the perfect 'brats'! Also to headmaster Kevin McMullen for letting us disrupt lessons to get the photographs taken. (The kids were more than grateful for that!)

| Introduction

ARE THEY REALLY BRATS?

We doubt that many people actually call them 'brats' to their faces . . . but it's certainly what a lot of people think! Every age is a difficult age and parents and youth leaders alike get totally frustrated with teenagers whether they're thirteen or nineteen years old, but young teens do have an awful lot to contend with. They are neither adults nor children, so we don't know how to treat them – and they don't know how they want to be treated! Wonderful, isn't it? In *The Brat Pack*, we hope to give some advice on talking, leading and being with eleven-to-fourteen-year-olds. There *will* be some ideas and things to do with them . . . but basically we would like to speak on their behalf and give you a little bit of insight into their world. Because most of us have probably blotted out the painful memories and the embarrassing things that happened to us during that time.

So, are eleven-to-fourteen-year-olds *really* brats? Of course they are! If you can't be a brat when you're twelve years old . . . when can you be? Everything you do is an experiment. What happens if I press this button? . . . If I shave this part of my head will I look more like a rebel? . . . If I shave part of the dog will he match my haircut?! . . . If I play-act that bit from the telly in front of my bedroom mirror will I look like a TV star? . . . These curtains really go well with my trainers . . .

There has to be a tremendous amount of give and take with

'The Brat Pack' because all the time that they are trying out these things, they are going to make dreadful mistakes. And when they do, the 'teenager' will dissolve into the frustrating tears of the 'kid' again. When this happens, we have to learn to give in to the side of the 'kid'. Our immediate reaction is to be extremely annoyed with the 'teenager', 'who should know better at his age' etc., etc., but then when we remember that this teenager is in fact only thirteen years old, we have to realize that they can't get it right all the time.

Often what they say to you comes from their own land of 'dreams and ambitions'. For instance, kids are always saying to John and me:

'When I leave school, I'm going to be in a rock band like you. I'm going to play a synthesizer and my mate Darren's gonna play the drums and Matt is our lead guitarist. We're only going to play in big clubs and venues – not schools like you – and we're gonna tour the world.'

'That's terrific!' say John and I. 'So how long have you been playing keyboards? It's great to start young and get together with your friends.'

'Oh I don't actually play anything yet . . .' is the standard reply, 'but I'm going to get one of the £2,000 keyboards with everything on it and then I'm gonna learn.'

'Oh, right.' We smile. 'So how about Darren and Matt?'

'Well, Darren's got a paper round so he's saving for some drums and Matt's next door neighbour's gonna learn him.'

You'll hear a lot more about these dreams in another chapter, but we have this kind of conversation in every school we play in (and we've played in well over fifteen hundred), and with every good intention in the world, they are going to do it! And not only that . . . but they are going to be the best there ever was – you wait and see! Unfortunately, next time you see them they're going to be Olympic athletes . . . just as soon as they've saved up £100 for the pair of trainers . . .

FICKLE MINDS

Being a youth leader for this age-group is a gamble, because they are liable to change their minds in mid-turn and leave you high and dry with fifty tickets for an ice hockey match that no one wants to see. This makes the task of encouraging them very difficult indeed . . . smiling whilst stuffing fifty tickets up a brat's nose is hard work!

I guess that you are beginning to get the message that working with this age-group is a God-given ministry, and if you're reading this book then I guess that ministry has been given to you. Please don't give up. It's a real pain but believe us, they need you more than you can imagine. Don't expect too many 'pleases' and 'thank yous' . . . but when they come, you'll really treasure the moment.

HOW MUCH DO YOU WANT TO HELP THEM?

When John was a pastor in the East End of London, we had a small church in Canning Town. One night, as we were locking up after a prayer meeting, a load of young teens came sauntering down towards us. Our church was in a cul-de-sac and we were at the bottom of it, and our first thoughts were that there was nowhere to run! These particular kids didn't look all that happy and they were coming straight for us! So we stood our ground and waited to see what was going to happen.

'You run this church?' one of them asked.

'Yeah,' we smiled.

'Got a youth club?' asked another one.

'No, we haven't,' we replied (well, we didn't have any young people, so it wasn't worth it).

One of the lads walked forward.

'Will you start one for us? We've been thrown out of all the others, and we haven't got anywhere to go.'

HOW COULD WE REFUSE?

Although there was only John and myself to run it (the rest of the church thought we'd lost our minds . . .), we decided to give it a shot. We didn't have a hall in our church, we just had one main building, so the youth club had to be started in the church itself. (The congregation, by now, were threatening to leave . . .)

So, once a week we had our youth club. We brought in a record player and some coffee, and that was it. We didn't have anything else to offer. The first few weeks were a nightmare, and the next few were just as bad. I used to be in the kitchen making coffee while John kept his eye on the record player and the thirty kids in the church. The first couple of times, hardly anyone spoke to us . . . they just sat around and chatted to each other. I suppose it was a bit like musical chairs really. I supplied the records (bought at a discount from the record shop I worked at), and then when the music stopped, that meant that all the records had been miraculously nicked from under our noses, and we all went home!

It took us weeks to work out how they were shifting the stuff, but eventually we saw the system. They were taking a record at a time, going to the loo and passing the record over the wall to someone waiting outside. (At least they liked our taste in music!) We decided to turn a blind eye to all this, and go with the flow.

THE BREAKTHROUGH

Quite a few weeks later, one of the girls from the club actually came and sat with me. 'I've got something for you,' she said. I grinned and wondered if she was going to present me with a stack of 45s. But she just stayed where she was and said:

'For God so loved the world that he gave His only Son, that whosoever believes in Him should not perish but have everlasting life.'

I was stunned. *'How did you know that?'* I marvelled.

She looked so matter-of-fact as she said, 'Oh, it's on a poster opposite my bus stop. I learnt it for you.'

Take my records! Take my record player! This was amazing! The next week, the girls offered to make the coffee. It was so brilliant!

I'm still convinced that if we had played the youth club another way, and told them off all the time, we would have become just another badge on their shoulder of places they'd been thrown out of. Like I said, when they say 'thank you' they say it with style!

You'll find an awful lot of this book has to do with actual events . . . things that have happened to us . . . conversations we've had . . . because that way we can prove to you that these things work!

Hopefully, as you read the chapters through, you will be encouraged to keep going with this age group. At the time of writing, Bart Simpson is one of their heroes . . . strange really that his first name is just an anagram of BRAT isn't it? . . .

CHAPTER TWO

The Kid Inside the Teenager

CUDDLY TOYS

There's a shelf in our bedroom piled high with fluffy toys. Edd the Duck and assorted penguins feature heavily. We are not 'cuddly toy' people . . . I'm more an earrings type and John is neither, funnily enough! And yet we get sent loads of this stuff. Our postman finds it all very amusing, as our letters often have coloured hearts and stickers on them – not to mention messages to the postman himself. Just this morning we received a letter from a young girl whose school we played in last week; the envelope was brilliantly covered in lightning streaks, hearts and stars. Each motif had been drawn by hand in different colours and must have taken for ever. The letter inside was much the same . . . multicoloured words written courtesy of a pack of felt pens.

It is important to recognize when a young person is reaching out to you.

When a young teenager is inspired by *anything* the chances are it will be written all over pencil cases and exercise books. Now I'd like to say that these kind of things happen just to girls who think soppy thoughts and daydream all the time. But it simply isn't true.

A few months ago we led a holiday club in Surrey. The hall we were given was large and bare and however much we tried to decorate it – it *still* looked large and bare. The eleven-to-fourteen-year-old kids at the club looked lost in this huge hall and so on the second day I said to them:

'Hey! How about bringing in your mascots and stuff and we'll sit them on the top of the speakers.'

I think that was the only time I mentioned it. The next morning, the queue outside looked like the line-up for *The Antiques Roadshow*. Our motley little crowd of kids were hugging any number of carrier bags and strange-looking objects.

When they came into the club, we were quite taken aback by the amount – but more importantly, the *types* – of mascots making their way to our speakers. There were loads of teddy bears, fluffy animals and trolls, plus the odd dinosaur and 'unidentifiable thing'. And I have to say that a large majority of these toys were brought in by thirteen- and fourteen-year-old boys. Fact.

Question 1: Why?

Question 2: *Why?*

Answer to the first question, I think, is that they are trophies. Each mascot probably reminds its owner of a special time in their life . . . and, sometimes sadly, it's something to cling to.

Answer to question 2 . . . They have no other way of telling you that they like you. To bring you a present, to them, is their greatest tribute. It doesn't come easy to kids to stroll up to anyone and say 'I like you.' I mean, yuk!

A TEENAGE CONVERSATION

We get letters from kids all over Britain, and sometimes we've written to them for years. (Oh yes, I'm sorry to make you feel guilty, but we *do* answer all their letters . . . eventually.) But, should we meet one of them face to face, they almost always clam up and don't say a word for ages. And yet in their letters they're saying things like: 'I'm writing this letter during English, what a bore! My friend says she really likes your clothes and Gemma says she doesn't believe you're a Christian because you look too trendy! When I go home tonight I've got loads and loads of homework, our geography teacher is mad . . .' etc., etc., Waffle waffle waffle. But as I said, face to face? Not a bean! So what are we expecting of them? An intellectual discussion?

Kids just don't make conversation in the same way an adult does. You have to make room for that.

This is the side of the teenager that is still a child. It is not to be mocked, it's very, very delicate and can easily be broken by misunderstanding their intentions.

A fourteen-year-old boy walked up to me at the end of Spring Harvest (a Christian Holiday Conference) and shoved a small fluffy penguin at me.

''ere you are,' said the gruff voice . . . and he walked away before I could say anything. Now, I could have completely embarrassed the life out of him by asking him what it was for. I could have shouted to the rest of the crew, 'Hey look, he's just given me a fluffy toy!' I could have even given it back to him saying 'No, you keep it.'

It was vitally important that I did none of those things. In fact I just nodded and smiled as he walked away. I knew it was more than likely that if he wanted any more contact, I would soon get a letter that started 'Hi, I'm the one who gave you the penguin . . .'

TAKE TIME TO WRITE.

Letters play a large part in the life of a teenager. When you're not quite old enough to be sure of your own feelings, it's easier to write them down than say them face to face. Letters are terribly important.

For example, when John and I embark on a week's schools work, we try to make sure that some kind of follow-up will be happening after we leave. It's always very painful to leave a load of kids behind not knowing if the organizers are actually going to cope. A while back we did a week's schools work and were asked to stay on for an extra week just to see the follow-up through. It was great and one of the things we had asked

8

the church to do was to send out letters to every kid who had responded in some way to the Christian message given out during our stay. The idea was that everyone who was spoken to after our main concert was told that they would receive a letter telling them of other events being put on especially for them. (So much better than expecting some kid to just turn up to a church service . . .) Well, all that week, we were meeting teenagers in the local town and they were coming up to us and saying 'I haven't had my letter yet!' The letter was more important to them than the event. As it happened the letters were all on their way – but it made us see just how important they were.

Taking time to write an invite or maybe just a few words of encouragement will mean a great deal to your kids. It can be a bigger tool in youth work than perhaps you realize.

We know that a lot of our replies to letters that come to our house are taken to school and shared amongst friends. We sometimes receive mail that has been written by any number of kids! They generally share the letter round during lessons or after school, and they all write a bit each.

I know letter-writing means you getting stuck in and very involved, but it's such a successful way of communicating. Generally we find that we leave a fair gap between the time we receive the letter and the time we answer it (unless it's urgent of course) because you can almost guarantee a response within four days.

HOLIDAY CLUBS

'The child inside the teenager' always comes to the surface during the summer for us. We are involved in lots of different holiday clubs – like the one in Surrey mentioned earlier. They tend to stick to a pattern of doing something for the seven-to-tens in the morning and something for the teenagers in the evening. A lot of the time, the main venue will be a marquee on a green, or a recreation ground in the middle of an estate. Once you've been established for a few days, you will notice a ritual that happens every day.

As soon as the children's programme starts, there will be a nucleus of older kids hanging around outside.

Causing trouble? No way . . . I mean if you treat them as if that's what you're expecting, that's what you'll get . . . no, they are just dying to get in on the fun that's happening inside the tent. There are *so many* kids who have reached their teens without ever having the experience of playing games as a child. Broken homes, unemployment, busy careers, life styles, have often taken over where the fun of being a child should have been. So there is still a great attraction in silly things like marshmallow games, team competitions and volunteering to have an egg cracked on your head.

Utilizing the older kids

As these guys were older, we couldn't really let them join in with a programme designed for smaller kids, so we decided to let them actually help with the running of the club. Some became group leaders, spurring their gang on and helping them cut things out and make models. The more artistic ones helped with face-painting and banners for the various teams. Because they were teenagers, they couldn't be seen to be playing children's games, but at least we could give them the next best thing!

Reactions often get in the way of what's really happening inside the teenager. It's important to take a second look at why someone is reacting in a certain way. Making a noise outside while you are trying to run a meeting, doesn't necessarily mean 'I am here to cause trouble' . . . it can simply mean 'Is there any room for people like me?'

Getting the games right

Playing games is a tricky situation. It's got to be done so that it's pitched just right. Too babyish and they won't join in . . . too college orientated and they'll think you're mad. And because humour is involved in most games, you've got to make sure you hit their funny bones too! We had a most embarrassing time with a leader who thought it was hilarious to get 300 kids to wander around wearing a badge with a cartoon picture on it. On the badge it said 'Who is Eric the Hedgehog?' And the kids kept asking him what the badges were for and he wouldn't tell them. He kept insisting that it was a lot of fun having people coming up to you and asking you what the badge was for . . . and then you had to look surprised as if *everyone* knew who Eric was. Then, on the last day, he got all the kids together and disclosed the great secret . . . Eric the Hedgehog didn't exist! Wasn't that a riot?

The kids were more than a little annoyed with him, and he couldn't understand that this prank may have been hilarious at some college with a load of off-beat students . . . but for a load of kids, it was rubbish. He also couldn't see why no-one entered his competition for 'colouring in your badge'.

If you find it difficult to pitch things at the right age group, then ask the kids themselves!

On the other hand, games can generally get as messy as possible before anyone complains. We've used some really foul games in the past and had kids queuing up to volunteer. One such competition included trampling a pound of grapes with your bare feet and then measuring the juice in two glasses to see who had the most 'wine'.

We also had a most wonderful 'spontaneous water fight' outside a church once. It just sort of happened, with one kid and a water pistol . . . then someone found a squeezy bottle . . . then the water balloons were brought in as reinforcements . . . and someone even went to a shop round the corner and bought two water cannons! Before we knew it, the whole thing included 'tactics' and 'plans' and it lasted for ages!

Well, once you're wet, you're wet, and there's very little damage involved in a soaking, but it's a lot of fun and the young teens don't find it at all childish.

Be prepared to drop those plans you've worked on for ages if something spontaneous happens. You can always keep your ideas for another week.

Teamwork

Young people don't like being singled out for things. It is the totally wrong age group for being 'pointed at' and 'picked on'. Belonging to a team gives them confidence and helps with their general enthusiasm.

The other thing that comes out of times like these, is teamwork. When peer pressure is such a problem, being in a team has great learning advantages. If you are a kid that's not so 'up front' then having a team to hide behind is wonderful. The child inside the teenager is quite happy to sit amongst a crowd of fifty or so kids, knowing he's safe . . . and the teenager in him feels confident to chant the team's name with his fist in the air with the others. Teams create excitement, they teach discipline and encourage enthusiasm at an age when everything around you is confusing.

They create a certain amount of confidence too – when your team wins you learn to cope with the highs, and when they lose you learn to cope with the lows. A young teen is normally at a loss when it comes to confidence, they aren't ready to cope yet with a lot of adult things we throw at them. In the last chapter of the book, we have let the 'brats' have their say, and one of the things that irritates them no end is when adults say to them 'Grow up! Act your age!' Because, believe me, that's exactly what they *are* doing!

SUMMARY

Accept their accolades gracefully.

Conversations can be hard for teenagers. Be aware of the signs that replace words . . . gifts, letters etc.

Many older kids have never played games. Give them space to experience fun.

Teamwork is preferable to anything that points them out individually.

CHAPTER THREE

The Sky's the Limit

W HAT did you want to be when you were at school? I wanted to be either a vet or a ballet dancer – John wanted to be a motorbike messenger! Neither of us are doing anything like we dreamed (in fact we surpassed our dreams long ago . . .) but it didn't hurt to have high hopes and ambitions.

John has always been a great believer in the five-year-plan. He has a huge list of things he wants to see happen in our lives over the next five years. Lots of people have laughed at this idea, but we both think it's important to keep thinking ahead. If you plan nothing . . . that's exactly what you'll get! So why not sort out what it is you want from life and aim for it? It works really well and we've encouraged loads of people to do the same. What do you want God to do in your life? What do you want to see happen? Well, in the last five years we must have gone through at least *three* of these plans, and it's only because we had something to aim at.

Kids have brilliant ideas on their future. Crazy, absolutely unreal ideas. Well, that's great, encourage them all you can. There's nothing worse than an empty life with no purpose and I know that if you look around you, you won't have to look far to see the results. So why crush someone's dream? *Teenagers have a hard enough life; it's up to you to help change that situation.*

In schools, young people are always telling us of their ambitions. We often ask them specifically, 'If you got all the right exams, and had the choice – what would you *really* like to do?'

14

The answers are varied but basically they all have one thing in common . . . to be a pop star, an airline pilot, appear on *Neighbours* . . . become a lawyer . . . a taster for Walkers crisps! Yes, they are all pretty unattainable without either a huge amount of qualifications, or a 'lucky break'. We've spoken to tons of kids who are convinced they will become world-famous stars, but if you ask them if they can play an instrument or sing, they will very seriously tell you that they can't – but they're 'going to learn because my friend's got a guitar the same as yours and his dad's friend knows someone in a record company . . .'

The fact that they can't play at the moment just doesn't come into it. The fact that there are 5,000 pop groups in London alone . . . and most of them are *good*, is neither here nor there. It's all irrelevant to a young person with high ideas.

TAKE TIME OUT TO LISTEN.

In the classroom we are often asked 'Are you going to put a song in the charts?' As if it's our choice. They have no conception of marketing, managers, venues, pluggers, agents, etc., they just look blankly at us and wait for the reply. As far as they are concerned, if we wanted a record in the charts, we could have one tomorrow . . . no problem!

Enthusiasm should always be encouraged, it's so rare! So maybe they won't become pop stars or airline pilots – but they'll have a lot of fun trying, and if they turn out to have a flair for that particular art, so much the better. Take it to the limit!

We know a young guy with a rare syndrome which makes studying very difficult for him. He's very likeable and a lot of fun, but slower than other kids of his age. However, his parents noticed that he had great rhythm. He would be forever tapping his hands to any kind of music, hitting boxes and upturned saucepans. So instead of stopping him, they encouraged him to try drumming. They bought him a small drum kit and sought out someone to give him lessons. As you can imagine, having a lad in the house whose complaint made him hard to handle, and *then* giving him a drum kit, was a brave thing to do, but they carried on, encouraging him as much as they could, and now Paul is a brilliant drummer. He drums for the worship band in his church and the last time I heard him he outshone just about every session drummer we've used in our studio! He's terrific, but if his parents hadn't encouraged him, it would have been an unused talent . . . a great shame.

Put your prejudices aside. It may not be *your* idea of progress, but it's not *you* that counts!

There are many other examples and sometimes you may think that their talents aren't worth encouraging, but you really have no idea how God can use these things. So let 'your young men see visions' – it's a very important part of growing up.

They need your help, but only when they can't do it themselves.

When I was young we had a youth club at a school, and we all went there every week. It was a real basic hut-type of thing with not a lot going for it. It was bare and not very comfortable, but it was ours. Then one day the youth leaders decided it was time to renovate it and were discussing what they were going to do. We were all horrified at the thought of our wonderful youth club being taken over by the 'older people' – until they turned to us and said, 'On the other hand, we could get the paint and brushes and you could do it yourselves.'

Now that was more like it! This was exactly the kind of thing we liked. It wasn't a case of 'You paint this with this colour.' It was just a case of 'It's your youth club, here's the stuff, we're over here if you want us.' And so we redecorated our youth club, and then when there were bits we couldn't handle, we happily went to our youth leaders and asked them to help.

THEIR FUN, YOUR RESPONSIBILITY

The same went for our carnival float. The youth club came up with the idea of decorating a float, they designed it and made all the props. The youth leaders did the difficult bits of hiring the lorry and sorting out the signing of forms and things, and we got on with the interesting stuff. And that's the way it should be. Kids shouldn't be responsible for the signing of the forms, that's *your* job. It's no good saying to them, 'If you want the fun, you have to have the responsibility' because they are only kids, and a thirteen-year-old kid should still be allowed to have some fun and not worry about the hassles.

There's a chapter in the book about how God uses teenagers all the time, and one of their main problems would be older people putting up stumbling blocks. We see the brick walls all too easily at times, whereas a young teen will only see the moon and the stars.

When the Lord made it blatantly obvious to us that we were to leave our church and tour around Britain in a Christian rock band, we had every possible stumbling block put in our way. Three of the guys in our band were only in their teens, but they really felt God touch their lives and they were raring to sell up, leave home, trust the Lord for money and leave the small island of Guernsey where we were living at the time. We absolutely knew that it was the right thing to do . . . but that didn't make explaining it to other people any easier! On the face of it, it could have been one big ego trip . . . rock band touring the world, fame and fortune. But we knew it wouldn't be like that, God had already specifically told us it would be hard, but that we would do more than we could even think about! Our enthusiasm to start this new step was unstoppable, and eventually the mocking slowed down and the sneers began to lessen. There was hardly a person who really encouraged us to step out and go for it. Most people told us to our faces that we would fail and it was all wrong, but we did it anyway – and seventeen years later God is still providing!

Encouragement would have been great at the time. So what if we'd fallen on our faces? At least we would have attempted something!

When a kid tells you a secret, a passion, something he's set his heart on . . . you must treat it with the greatest respect.

So when some kid opens his heart to you and says he's going to be a star . . . encourage him. Suggest someone you know who could give him a few guitar lessons. (He'll soon give up after the first week if he doesn't like it.)

When kids are just toddlers, you encourage them to run and jump and play, and then when they fall over and hurt themselves, you pick them up and nurse the grazes.

Young teens are exactly the same. You encourage them to have a go at some crazy ambition, and if they don't make it, you pick up the pieces and encourage them to start something else!

DON'T LIMIT THEM.

Once they have an idea in their heads, young people will go to great lengths to put it into action, in their own way. On TV recently there was a young girl who had turned her garden into a nature reserve – it was absolutely fabulous! She loved animals and wildlife (happily that's a very common state in young people) and decided to give it her best shot. Her garden was such a success that well-known and authoritative naturalists were paying visits to talk to her and then she found herself on TV! I'm sure if she had told her parents what she was going to achieve, they would have been like the rest of us, saying 'Oh yes, how nice.'

If this is how an average teenager daydreams and goes about life, then surely we must see great possibilities with our Christian kids! If we can inspire them, they could take off! When I first became a Christian, I just wanted to tell everyone and it never occurred to me that they might not want to listen. Admittedly I was older (twenty-one in fact), but even so, I had ambition. I chatted to people on my train on the way to work, I got out of the car at traffic lights to hand people leaflets explaining what they were missing, I painted my denim jacket with Christian slogans and wore a massive cross on a leather cord around my neck – I was going to save the world!! I had not the first idea about anything when it came to Christianity, I only knew I wanted to be an outspoken Christian who wasn't going to hide in a building. We must encourage young Christians at all cost, even when they have stars in their eyes and their ambitions seem way off beam.

I mean, what would have happened if Billy Graham's youth leader had discouraged *him*?

SUMMARY

Don't crush the dream.
Listen to their crazy ideas.
Encourage the enthusiasm.
Their fun, but your responsibility.
Help all you can, but leave some of it in their hands.

Hero Worship

EVERYONE has heroes. It's part of life. Don't tell us you never had a hero – we don't believe you! The need to model yourself on someone when you're young is essential, it's part of growing up. When you haven't yet found your own identity, you need someone else's for a while. It doesn't have to be someone famous, a lot of the time it's someone at school who's a bit older than you, or maybe someone who's just a lot louder.

You must keep putting yourself in their place.

I got in with the 'wrong crowd' when I was at school. I had bags of potential, but my head was firmly turned by our little group. There was Pauline, the quiet one who liked horses and knew nothing about anything else, Janet who said lots but did nothing, Terry, the actress (unfortunately we looked fairly similar and were forever getting told off for each other's dastardly deeds!) and Kathy, the ringleader, destined to have fifty million boyfriends by the time she was fourteen. The word serious was not in Kathy's dictionary. Then there was me, curly hair, big eyes and slightly innocent.

When we all got together we were such a terrible pain. It must have been just the right blend of everything to create havoc. Kathy and Terry would usually hatch the plot, Janet and I would look too innocent to have been involved in 'such a thing', and Pauline would take the blame! Together we were loud and fearless, looking down on everyone else and mocking them mercilessly if they dared try to be 'like us'.

Now, get one of us on our own and you'd probably see us all

in a different light – except Kathy. She would still be loud and abusive to any teacher, even if we weren't there to back her up. So I guess she was our role model.

Even in those days (oooh, listen to her!) it was important to be seen doing the right thing and wearing the right thing. We had a very strict school uniform and yet it still caused endless problems for kids and parents alike. There was a phase we all went through of wearing paisley scarves under our coats . . . and even though they were under our coats, they had to bear the label of 'Tootal'. Tootal scarves were expensive and the kind of thing that my family couldn't afford to dish out on. They were also men's scarves, so you had to go into a posh bloke's shop to buy one. This fashion was one of my 'glory' times. My dad had one! He wore it for work every day . . . well, until I found it anyway. I was the only one in our gang that had one, and I can still remember how good it made me feel!

I was also the proud owner of a pair of mock-alligator-skin boots (don't get too excited!). We were only allowed regulation shoes at school, but this was the school Christmas party and we could wear whatever we liked. My boots were a sensation . . . but what the girls didn't know was that the next day my mum took them back to the shop because they cracked, and they were swapped for a 'sensible' pair instead!

When you are a young teenager it's so important not to stand out from the crowd! You want to be like someone else – or everyone else for that matter! So it would probably help if we didn't harp on so much about kids having to 'make a stand' for Jesus . . . it would be much better to let them see Jesus as a kind of hero, someone they want to like and imitate. Jesus is a great person to want to be like, so that in itself should be a much easier route than the 'stand out in a crowd' routine.

It's all about being sensitive.

Do you remember secretly styling yourself on someone? Girls in their teens have all, at some time or other, stood in front of a mirror with a hairbrush and sung into it. When there's nobody in, the tape gets put on a high volume, the hair is styled in a way that your mum would kill you for, you drag the sheet off the bed and wrap it round you as if it were some terrific stage costume . . . and away you go! Even better if your friends come round and the mirror's big enough!

Boys, apparently, do the same kind of thing when they are running errands down to the local shops. They start dashing about at great speed and kick at a stone/Coke can/any old rubbish, and in their heads they hear the commentary 'and he passes the ball, look at him go, the ball comes back and he's there with a tremendous flick . . . the ball sails across and YES! It's there! What a goal! The crowd go wild!'

Everyone has a hero. In Britain, you can virtually guess who people admire by their attitude and the way they dress. If you are a heavy metal freak, then the chances are you will wander around with long permed hair, a black tee shirt complete with 'metal' slogans, and pair of ripped jeans and a black leather jacket. If on the other hand you are into hi-tech and dance stuff, you'll wear designer clothes and million-pound trainers. The clothes and the music go hand in hand and have to be seen together. Strangely enough, this doesn't seem to be the trend in Europe, where a rave fanatic is just as liable to wear black tee shirts and leather jackets, and a heavy metal fan is happy in a baseball cap and sweat-shirt. It's different wherever you go . . . and yet it's the same . . . people want to look like they belong.

As a youth leader, stand back and admire their clothes and music, etc. They don't want you to look like them, but – hopefully – they *will* want to *be* like you.

Before you are a teenager, you tend to look at your family as your role model, but as soon as you start to grow, you look outside that circle and your friends start to affect your attitudes, your jargon and your dress sense. Words that your parents have never heard you use before become a common part of your vocabulary, and the four set answers to every question become your way of life. 'Don't know', 'Nowhere', 'But' and 'Boring'.

LOOK OUT FOR YOUNG CHRISTIANS . . . Help them grow by making it easier for them.

A Christian kid has it hard at this stage. He has all this to contend with, and the life he has had at home so far. If the parents are Christians, then this is normally a time when he starts to question the whole thing for himself:

'Do I believe in this stuff? Or is it something I just know about?'

'Do I want Jesus to have an influence on my teenage life, or should I listen to this other stuff my new friends are telling me about?'

It is a crucial decision-making time, and I think we should make it as easy for them as possible. The young teen has met a wall head-on and our glib answers of 'because it's true' and 'because the Bible says so' are no longer good enough. There have to be reasons, good reasons, and this is exactly when making your own decision is earth-shatteringly important. No kid is going to survive in school, with his friends, at the local hang-out place, if all he has going for him of Christianity is that his parents have told him it's right. He *has* to know Jesus for himself if it's ever going to get him anywhere.

JESUS AS A HERO

If your hero is the lead singer of Guns 'n' Roses, then you will collect their records, have posters on your wall, you will save like crazy to buy tickets for their concerts and you will meet up with other fans just to talk about how great they are. That's fine.

If Jesus is supposed to be your hero . . . then somewhere along the line people are going to wonder where the signs are. Do you read any Christian books? Were you in the front row running down the High Street when March for Jesus came to your town? Are you looking forward to the next time you and your Christian friends get together? If the answer to these questions is 'no' . . . that's OK, at least it's a starting point. You can't have Jesus as a hero until you know him for yourself. This is where parents have to opt out and let kids make up their own minds. You can't become a Christian for someone else.

To give your life to Jesus when you are a young teenager is a terrific start . . . if you know what you are doing. Because you will have confidence in that Jesus figure that you hear other people talk about.

Listen, youth worker. Kids have a hard enough time as it is; please try and be sympathetic to their cause, don't belittle their heroes but try to encourage them as much as you can.

It is possible to admire a heavy metal band, to wear designer-label clothes and have posters of Beverley Hills 90210 all over the bedroom . . . and still be a Christian. It's just a matter of getting it all into perspective and making sure that in order of importance . . . Jesus is Number One.

SUMMARY

Keep thinking back to how you felt at that age.
Take time to admire their style.
You can't become a Christian for someone else . . .
they have to make their own decision.
Hero worship is fine, in perspective.

CHAPTER FIVE

Common Ground

K EEP *checking your own knowledge of young people.*
At the first year of a youth leaders' conference called 'Brainstormers', John and I took some seminars on the Brat Pack age group. We devised what we thought was a simple test, almost for fun really. It comprised of around twenty questions about things kids would be interested in. Such as: Who's number one this week? What's the major story in *Neighbours* at the moment? Name two popular makes of trainers, etc., etc. We gave the papers out to around a hundred youth leaders and were amazed at their reactions. Some actually gave the papers back and said they were 'not cut out to be a youth leader', others were more horrified that they didn't actually know the answers! It was a real eye-opener for us because we just hadn't expected these reactions at all. Quite a few leaders laughed at the thought of being able to give the correct answers to such questions.

But when you think about it, if you were looking after animals, you would be expected to know what they liked to eat, what their habits were and how they generally liked to be treated, wouldn't you? If you worked in a bank, they'd expect you to be able to add up. If you're a marriage guidance counsellor, you may even have been on courses to learn how to handle people in distress . . . so what's so terrible about knowing how to handle the Brat Pack?

So what do you need to know? How should you be reacting? *You must let the kids see the real you.*

There is probably nothing worse than a youth leader *trying* to be trendy. If you *are* a trendy person, that's OK, but if you're not . . . don't be. Kids are not daft, they see you for what you really are and no amount of pretending will ever take them in – but it *will* put them off!

BE PROUD OF THEIR ACHIEVEMENTS.

This week we've been working in a coffee bar type of place, where kids come in off the streets and spend some time playing snooker and sitting around eyeing up the talent. One of the ladies that helps out there looks like 'everybody's mum', and she's very popular. Why? Because she really likes the kids and takes them at face value. The rougher kids spend time talking to her because they know she understands why their only defence is to hit out now and again. She was telling us of a boy recently who had something stolen by another kid who was just as bad as he was. 'I'm so proud of him,' she said. 'The other boy gave him a real shiner, and he didn't retaliate. You know, he could have leathered the other kid into the ground, but he walked away.' She understood.

TAKE TIME to list your own talents.

So what do you have in common with the kids you work with or talk to each week? You do need to have something they can relate to . . . that lady had an insight into the kind of background those kids had come from, but it could be anything. Let's have a look, remembering that some of the things I'm writing about now could be well out of fashion by the time you read this!

Music: What do you listen to? Music is probably the biggest communicator there is, so if you like the same music as the kids, then you have a common interest. But it has to be real! There's absolutely no point in pretending you like the music just because you think you should. On the other hand you may be able to play an instrument. In the summer we worked with a youth group where one of the leaders was a drummer. So, while everyone else played volleyball, etc. outside, he gave drumming lessons to the kids inside. Obviously, this was a big hit as loads of young teens wouldn't normally get the chance to *see* a drum kit, let alone sit behind one!

Another guy working in Hertfordshire takes his drums into a local school and takes around thirty lessons a week. So instruments can play a large part in youth work. And of course, if you have the time and patience . . . you'll find yourself with a band on your hands before you know it!

If you're not into pop music, it's a good idea to tell the kids and confess you don't know the first thing about it – and if you're a real hero, you can take it one step further and insist that *they* teach *you*! Ask them (nicely . . . !) if you can sit in while they watch a TV music programme, or get them to play their favourite records to you. Ask decent questions, and you'll find they'll enjoy educating you!

But – and this is a very big but – don't ever down it! There is absolutely no mileage in scorning and putting down something that's very important to them.

Sport: On the other hand, you might be a very sporty person. The field does narrow down a bit now, but there's plenty of interest in leisure sports like tenpin bowling, ice-skating and five-a-side football. Along with this you may find you have a local Christian sportsman able to give you a hand now and again. And as with the drummers mentioned earlier, perhaps you are good enough yourself to give lessons. An American youth leader we know regularly gives basketball lessons, and the kids really look up to him in more ways than one!

Computers: . . . ah, yes, there's so much that can be done in this technological age of ours. John and I can think of yet another youth leader who's tone deaf, useless at sport, but terrific when it comes to computers. I don't know how he did it, but at his youth club he linked up loads of TVs and keyboards and had a whole row of tables filled with computer games! The kids loved it, and the type of games were up to him and the length of time they played was up to him too, but because of his own interest in computers, he was able to gain a lot of ground with his youth group.

The same type of boffin can be found building video walls and teaching kids to use soldering irons and make their broken electronics work again.

Environment: Pretty endless really. Gardening, nature walks, birdwatching. People are always surprised when they find that John and I enjoy birdwatching. But, you see, we were first taken out on a trip by a very enthusiastic Christian who introduced us to this special hobby. He made us appreciate God's handiwork, His creation and told us how he sees birdwatching as a form of worship! Now there's a thing! Next time you tell the youth group that you're taking them out for a time of praise and worship . . . try going on a nature walk!

I hope by now you will have found the place where you fit in. I've only covered a few here, but you know what you're good at, so get in there and share it with the kids. When you're genuinely interested in something, it tends to be infectious, and that has to be a good thing.

MUTUAL INTERESTS ARE YOUR KEY CARD

Common ground is your entry to so many other important things. It's not so hard to have some kind of discipleship courses going, if you've first joined in a decent game of five-a-side with the disciples in question! Sharing their interests means that they will begin to share yours. Make Bible study something enjoyable, for yourself as well as the kids you are teaching. You have a lot to give and the kids have a lot to learn – and believe us, they *do* want to learn!

We were invited to go and talk to a youth group in Surrey last year. We were informed that not many of the group actually went to church, but they all gathered afterwards in the church hall opposite. So we went along and after the service we were shown across the road to one of the world's tattiest halls. It had nothing going for it. Nothing at all. It was completely bare, no carpet, some chairs, bare walls . . . not even a cassette player in the background to welcome people as they arrived. So all in all, it was everything we didn't want. John and I sat at the front and waited for the dribble of young people to arrive.

The doors opened and within five minutes there must have been 150 teenagers crammed into this hall! It was an amazing sight. Most of them were very trendy and good-looking – and we couldn't for the life of us understand what they were doing in the tiny church hall. So we immediately fell on the youth leaders and asked them what their secret was! It *had* to be something outstanding, and we wanted to be in on it.

THE QUALITY OF A GOOD YOUTH LEADER

How can I describe these leaders to you? Ordinary? Young married couples? People-next-door-type? Sainsbury shoppers? There were around six of them, and they all shrugged their shoulders and confessed that they had no idea why they attracted this great crowd.

'But what do you *do* with them?' we asked.

'Well, we normally sing some choruses and then one of us talks to them about the Lord and then we split up into small groups and discuss what's been said,' they replied.

The actual answer to our question is twofold:

1 Teenagers really are interested in knowing about God. They are inquisitive about this person Jesus, but not many people are telling them what they want to know.
2 A crowd attracts a crowd. This little spot had become the greatest dating agency in the town! Once you manage to get

above a certain number of kids, they start to swarm in. It becomes 'the place to be' . . . and the fact that it's a naff church hall with no facilities is irrelevant!

All the way through this book, we hope to encourage rather than put you off . . . and in this particular case, it was definitely 'If they can do it – we can do it!' It was a terrific encouragement to see this Bible study group having such a huge impact on a large percentage of the teenagers of one small town! So don't despair if you think your youth leaders are too 'mumsy' or too 'boring' . . . start writing out a list of things that you like and don't like. Things that you are good at. And then move on those   things . . . and watch the Lord move on everything else!

SUMMARY

A genuine interest in their hobbies will take you into their confidence.
Be proud of your young people.
List your interests and find the common ground.
Be yourself. Young people will see through a sham.

CHAPTER SIX

Youth Club Versus the 'God Slot'

Y OUTH clubs. What do you think they are really for? The title suggests that it's a place where kids go to meet each other and hang around chatting, maybe having the odd game of table tennis. Yet a lot of the time we use them as yet another place to get the Gospel over . . . and for once, I wonder if that is actually not such a tremendous idea?

We need to think things through to the final result.

Youth clubs really are where kids meet because there's nowhere else to go, it's cheap and they can stand around watching each other play snooker, eye up the talent and spend all their money at the tuck shop. It's almost a sort of 'safe house' for a lot of kids. Quite a few youth club workers have told us of the frustration of not getting in more than one type of kid, but quite honestly, there's only a certain type of kid that *enjoys* youth clubs. They are the ones that don't get much attention at home, the ones who are kicked out straight after tea and have nothing else to do. There is an enormous number of young teens who have missed out on their age-group . . . they've never played at home with their brothers and sisters, they've never sat and had a laugh with their mum and dad . . . home for them is not a place you look forward to going to.

But at the youth club there are these leaders who play football with them, they challenge them to a game of badminton and they tease them about the girls they fancy. There's usually some music on if you just want to sit and chat, and you only get yelled at if you break a snooker cue and that's your own fault anyway.

In other words, it's an ideal situation for that type of kid, and depending on the social scene in your area, you'll either get a lot of them, or just a few – but you can almost guarantee that if you delve into the backgrounds, they'll be very similar to the one I've suggested. Most of your youth club members will be off the streets. (Church kids don't normally frequent these places unless they are 'helping'.) Now, because of this, they need special care and attention.

THE GOD SLOT

What John and I are convinced they *don't* need is a compulsory 'God Slot' five minutes before closing time. Wince, wince . . . yes, you know what I mean. There *has* to be a better way of sharing Jesus with these kids than making it such a stipulation that it becomes a threat.

'If you don't attend the God Slot, then your membership is shot and you can't come any more till next term.'

Can you think of a worse way to introduce anyone to Christianity!? This obligatory five minutes is murder for everyone. We have met so many youth workers who despair of it and yet can't think of any way round it if they want to carry on calling it a Christian Work.

Well, we think that a youth club is a place where you work on relationships. It's a place where one-to-one is a priority. There are plenty of ways to show Christianity to people and in this particular situation the words 'Salt and Light' come heavily to the forefront. If God is a reality in your life, then this is the place it needs to shine. Maybe it's easier to shout at kids for five minutes a week and feel that 'at least you tried', but the real hard work is getting out there and letting all your life show Jesus and His love. The positive and effective reality of Jesus in your life will count for a thousand God Slots in this venue. We have done hundreds of these compulsory spots and the look of resentment on the faces of the youth is enough to make you realize it's a non-starter. There's no way round it. You might as well say to the kids, 'OK, that's enough fun, now we are going to ruin it all by making you listen to some boring speech by someone who doesn't want to do it anyway.' We know that nearly every one of you feels the same on this score – so why do we keep doing it?

ALTERNATIVE WAYS

Let's check some other ideas:

Instead of an agonizing five minutes that seems like five hours every week, why not just do something a bit more constructive once a month? This way you have much more time to draw on what it is your want to put over, and a month to prepare something special. Remember most of these kids don't go to church, so you must bring things down to their level. Use local performers, maybe a drama group or a video presentation that they will make sense of. Don't run it for five minutes . . . run it for twenty! The normal God Slot is just what it says it is . . . a slot that is shoved in to fill in a few minutes, not worth anything much, not worth bothering about really.

Try to put the presentation in the *middle* of the evening, so that the kids realize that they can go back to playing table tennis when it's finished. It's not the end, it's not the boring bit, it's in the middle while they are drinking their Cokes and eating crisps . . . it's a bit of a break from the snooker to watch a couple of entertaining sketches.

Once you have run this kind of programme for a few months, it might be an idea to try an even bigger event once every six months. Find out if there is anything large in the Christian scene happening around your area, and see if you can persuade the organizers to bring the band and lights, etc.

into your club one night. If not, try organizing a trip out to a Christian concert or something. Just the fact that it's a ride in the minibus and a bit of a laugh will help.

Once you have established these kind of events with your youth club, you can move on to taking them on weekends away. There's a whole chapter about them later in the book, but basically, taking away a group of kids who have now got some smattering of Christian teaching, is a great step forward. The weekends are a lot of fun, high on activities with some light teaching thrown in. It's a brilliant time to let the kids get together with their own thoughts, without the interruption of home life, school, etc., getting in the way. For many of them, it will be heaven on earth; they will be free to laugh and cry, to examine and test, to experiment with prayer without anyone pointing at them.

MAKING PROGRESS

On the last weekend we did (last week!), I asked one fourteen-year-old lad if he had been on a weekend before, and his reply was 'No, and I've only been here an hour but I absolutely love it and I'm coming again next year!' Progress can be made, but as usual it takes more effort on the part of the youth worker to make it happen. Most of the time the team of workers is made up of youth leaders, some church people who can cook and a guest who is brought in to provide the spiritual influence. Now, here's a chance to invite whoever has been the most successful visitor to your youth club! So the kids have already met him or her and realize he or she is no big threat to them. And when you come back, don't forget to make a huge poster to stick on the wall, of all the photos and mementos of the holiday. *The club members will pore over them for ages* and tease each other about 'the time Alex fell in the river' and how 'one of the leaders had to sleep outside the dorm in a sleeping bag because it was the only way to shut the lads up!'

Any members of your club that didn't go are almost bound to put their names down for the next one straight away, and you will find yourself in a very popular position. We know of some leaders who take their kids away as many as four times a year! That's a lot to handle, but it does show how popular these events are with youth club kids.

SUMMARY

The youth club situation should not be looked on so evangelistically.
Treat it as a space-maker.
Drop the God Slot and concentrate on bigger events.

CHAPTER SEVEN

Hi-Tech?

TECHNOLOGY has come a long way in the past few years, and the fact that kids are probably way ahead of anyone else in their interest in the whole spectrum means that *youth leaders have to keep up*. It's not just the computer side of things, it's the fact that everything today is professional. Kids have keyboards in their bedrooms that can be programmed to mimic their own voices, to provide accompaniment to anything they fancy learning to play. They can tell the keyboard to memorize what they've just played and then play it back with totally new sounds . . . in fact it does everything but make toast. Computer games come in fantastic colours, with little tunes that are so strong they are making the charts! They can see *Neighbours* by tuning in their wristwatches and dial a freefone number on their parents' cellphone to talk to Esther Rantzen.

How on earth are you supposed to keep up with that?

We've mentioned, in another chapter, the work we do in schools, and these days music teachers are eternally grateful to us for coming in to their lessons and showing the kids what MIDI is all about. (Musical Instrument Digital Interface! . . .) It's part of the school curriculum and has to be taught but, let's face it, if you are a music teacher who has majored on acoustic instruments such as the piano and violin, then there is no way you can just pick up the whole spectrum of electronic music – you've almost got to go back to school yourself.

Don't be too ambitious too soon.

So how can *you* take advantage of it all?

First of all, I think, by keeping within certain limits. If you are not technically minded, then it's best not to get too ambitious straight away. We've watched people get out of their depth with smoke machines and video walls, ambitious multi-effect programmes, and it's not worth it. It just makes you look very unprofessional. So let's take a look around at what's available and realistic:

Using a microphone brings more out of young people.

Microphones . . . We have stressed time and time again in this book that the use of a microphone at your event or youth meeting will alter the whole feel. People take you much more seriously when you have a mike in your hand, and then discussions and get-togethers can swell into much more. We spend a lot of our time asking kids questions, using a mike. General questions like 'Who's your favourite band?' and 'Where would you like to go on holiday?' get a much better response than usual. Instead of 'Haven't got one' or 'Nowhere', you are much more liable to get not just the answer, but all the reasons why as well. For kids, talking into a mike and seeing people using mikes is normal. They see it every moment on TV, and it works. They see phone-ins and kids interviewing pop stars . . . that's the way it's done these days.

Share the presenting.

The other thing they are used to seeing is two people compering the programme. Use this, it's a great way of sharing the load. Don't do bits each . . . be up there together, chatting to each other as well as the kids. It creates a good relaxed atmosphere for your young people to slip into.

A microphone will hold their attention, which, if you are a normal youth leader, will be very good news for you!

JINGLES AND BACKGROUND MUSIC

This is definitely one of the areas where people get themselves into a right old mess. Jingles are a very ambitious idea in the first instance, and are the absolute pits if they go wrong. If you plan a programme around some taped jingles, you are liable to come unstuck very easily. Jingles are great fun to make. Get yourself a twin tape deck or a four-track cassette recorder and you're there . . . the trouble starts afterwards. There is hardly a sound engineer alive who can press a PLAY button at the right time. If he does, you can almost guarantee that the tape isn't lined up properly. It's frustrating, you have spent days recording two little jingles . . . one that goes 'It's time for the Money Game!' with a bit of music behind it, and one that is just music to introduce guests, etc. So you are on stage and you say, 'Please will you give a big hand for our guest musician Gary Bendricks!' – then there's a big nothing, and as Gary comes to the mike to say hello – the jingle plays!! You see, most jingles are only four or five seconds long, and that's all it takes to walk across a stage or hall, so if they are not lined up to the minutest detail, they will be late, come in halfway or not at all. Whichever happens, it looks bad and you go way down in the estimation of the kids you want to please.

Make use of talents in your youth group.

Don't worry, there is a way out. Remember that kid I told you about, with his keyboard that makes toast? Now, *that* is what you're after! You get the kid to programme in a few little tunes with perhaps a drum rhythm and then he brings it along to your event. Now, his programmes are numbered on his keyboard. So, if he pushes 38 and hits PLAY, he gets instant access to that tune. So, all he has to do is look at the running order of your programme and make sure he has the right number punched in ready. *Then* the minute you announce something, he hits PLAY, *and it's there!* Wonderful, no hassles and, even better, some of your young people have been needed to help put the programme together! Great, eh? There is another way of providing music by way of background and for games to make them more exciting . . .

THE USE OF A WALKMAN

When John and I organize a game for a load of kids, you will usually find that as soon as we say 'Go!' music appears as if from nowhere and the game has much more excitement to it. We have literally been inundated with people asking us where they can buy the little controls that we use for our music. They see us walking around with a small box attached to a very long lead and assume that we are triggering off some clever device that's playing the music. However, it's much more simple than that. The 'magic box' is a Walkman. An ordinary Walkman with a lead attached. The lead is a mini-jack that fits into the headphone socket and a mono-jack that fits into our mixer or amplifier. Most radio/TV-type shops will sell you a lead like this, and if they haven't got one, they will make one up for you.

The next secret with this 'mystery music' is that we record cassettes especially for it. It's almost imperative to do it this way because when you buy a tape, no matter how good it is, it will generally have two things wrong with it. One, there will be gaps in between the songs (which means gaps just when you don't want them in the middle of some item), and two, there will be the inevitable slow song. *You need a whole cassette of fast-moving music that never lets up*, that way you won't get caught out *wherever* you turn it on.

The simple ideas are always the best, so why complicate things?

VIDEOS – A HELP OR A COP-OUT?

Videos are probably one of the biggest boons to modern-day media! There is nothing that can't be said by video, and usually it's told a thousand times better because you can make a video programme do just about anything. Video has come on in leaps and bounds . . . seeing is not believing any more, because you can edit anything to your liking and make it look totally believable. (See *Terminator*!!)

Now, there are a few ways to use the video and TV screen with a youth group, and the worst way is to stick a film on and use it as a way of not preparing your youth meeting. There are times when just getting kids to watch a film is great – but you really have to examine *why* you are doing this. Sometimes people ask John and me to take an 'informal' youth meeting, so that we can get to know the kids in an unpressurized situation. Now, we know that if you decode this message it means 'while you're here doing all this other work, could I off-load my lot onto you as well?'

Entertainment and relaxation

Now, *this* is a great time to use a video! We've been dropped in it and the youth leader has nothing prepared . . . so we normally try to make a good evening out of it, by getting the kids together and finding out what film they would like us to go out and rent for the evening and then we raid the youth club's 'tuck money' and splash out on Coke and popcorn all round. We hunt around the church building for the comfiest chairs, and beanbags from the children's room, and try to make the evening as relaxed as possible. If you're going to spend the evening watching a video . . . you might as well do it right!

However, there are much better ways of using it, so we'll discuss a few of those.

The starting point for teaching

Videos are often used as a *part* of a programme, rather than the be-all and end-all of it. If you are taking a subject and need to get a few points over, start thinking of pieces of film that you've seen that would help. I will mention some here that might be well out of date by the time you read this book, but at the same time you should be able to recall and understand. For instance, if you are using the environment as your topic, then there is a great video called *Creature Comforts* that you can use. 'Creature Comforts' are probably most well-known for their Electricity adverts on TV. The guy who 'invented' these fabulous characters is a Christian, as it happens, and the video has short sketches using these wonderful Plasticine animals.

There is one particular sketch where the animals are enclosed in their cages and special confinements of a zoo, and they talk about what it's like to be cooped up all day. The whole thing is done with a great sense of humour; it is like a spoof-documentary with polar bears lying around saying things like 'I don't get out these days as much as I like. The flat isn't bad, but when you've got the kids running round all day, you feel a bit closed in.' Baby polar bears are adding their little bits, and it's utterly charming. The idea, of course, is to make you think and it does this most effectively. It's a great runner into a discussion.

Use what is available.

Recently, when talking about schools with a load of kids, we used the video *Take That and Party*. (It's irrelevant here that the group Take That may not exist any longer . . . but at the time they were the bee's knees . . .) The film consists of the group's latest songs plus some talky bits in between, and one of the things they discuss is what they were like at school. Love it or hate it, *young people would rather hear what other young people feel about the subject*, and will take more note of *how their heroes feel*, than how *you* feel! Sorry. Anyway, in this particular video they happen to talk about bullying, school reports and whether R.E. is a waste of time. So again, it's a great way to use a video because it helps the discussion you are trying to promote. There are now Christian video libraries which will provide you with a decent catalogue of latest films. So mix and match! *Just make sure everything is lined up before you start your programme* ... there's nothing worse than psyching all the kids up, then pressing PLAY and getting fuzzy dots or the wrong piece! Believe me, we know!

Video walls

Ambitious things like a 'video wall' should be left to the experts! There are people who will come and do all that for you, and it's a fascinating thing to use for a large mission, or a town-wide youth event. If you *are* thinking of trying something yourself, we played at a youth club where they had actually bought about twelve old colour TVs – in various states of battered condition but all working – and literally built their own! It was a bit precarious playing our music in front of the 'wall' wondering if at any moment it was going to come thundering down on top of us!

They had wired all the TVs together and connected them to one video recorder, so while we played, they showed a video behind us on twelve different screens! After the break, they came back with a camcorder and relayed our performance on to the screens while we played ... and then turned it on the audience so that they could watch themselves dancing and singing away. As with most things, kids like to hear or see other kids taking part, which is why the next part of 'how to use video in your youth programme' is important!

Using a camcorder

Everyone knows someone with his own camcorder, and this lends itself to your group doing anything from a silly game to an out–and–out production! We've seen some wonderful ones lately.

Video your youth event. One we particularly liked started life at a 'Lock In' . . . for the unitiated, a Lock In is a hideous idea thought up by a madman, of getting all your young people together in the church hall from 9 p.m. on Saturday night until 9 a.m. on Sunday morning. The main idea is that you keep awake for the whole time! Games, seminars, treasure hunts, and loads of videos were heavily involved in this . . . and if you've ever tried to deliver a seminar at three o'clock in the morning to a load of kids who think they are still awake . . . you will know what a load of fun it all is!!!

Well, anyway, on this particular one, they had the terrific idea of videoing the leaders taking the Sunday Service from their beds. The idea was that by Sunday morning they would all be much too tired to attend the service, so if they videoed themselves leading it they could just stick a TV on in the church, and the service would run itself! Laugh, you may . . . but it worked amazingly well!

The congregation came into church to be greeted by TV screens on either side of the aisles. When everyone was there, the TV screens came alive and showed two youth leaders asleep in bed. They gradually woke up and scratched their heads, looked up at the screen, grinned and apologized for not being there in person! They then went on to announce the first hymn, which the bemused congregation stood up and sang! The whole thing was incredibly well done, and nobody took offence. Gradually more things started to happen . . . one of the leaders realized that he should be singing a song in the programme and leapt out of bed and hurriedly put a suit on over his pyjamas. He rushed out of the room and the screen went blank . . . just as he appeared from the vestry still doing up his tie! So now you had video plus the real thing! At the end of the song, the video came back on again and we watched the youth reading the notices from various famous landmarks in their local area. Sketches that had been rehearsed during the Lock In were performed 'live' as the kids appeared too. The whole service was a great success – yes, it was hard work for the whole youth team, but they threw themselves into it and the congregation was very appreciative of all this initiative! (Well done, Thundersley!)

When we were writing the chapter on Youth Weekends, I was reminding you to take photos of events for the kids to show at school, but of course a video of *What We Did At Camp* is also a good idea.

There is no end of uses for a camcorder, and I think that every youth group should at least have its own TV and video recorder. Get on to it, youth leaders, it's almost essential these days! We know of several youth groups who have collected petrol coupons to purchase video material for their church. If you get your whole church buying their petrol from the same type of station, you'll get your cassette player in no time. In fact, we know of one group who managed to get a petrol station involved, and they had a poster up asking people who didn't use their coupons to put them in the box provided . . . and they got their TV and recorder and had enough left over to purchase a minibus!!!!

True!

So don't just sit there! The kids will only get enthusiastic if you do. Use technology, it will give you more credibility and it's an attractive way of sharing the Gospel.

SUMMARY

Keep in touch with developments in communication technology.
Be as professional as possible.
Get a co-presenter to help you.
Make use of the talents in your youth group.
Avoid video cop–outs.
Don't be overambitious and make a fool of yourself.
Better, do something simpler but professional.

CHAPTER EIGHT

On the Right Wavelength

C AN you remember being told that you were at an 'awkward age'? Didn't it make you feel like you were from another planet? But the trouble is, it's true! People say that early teens are a terribly awkward age.

(Are they awkward, or are you just not reading them right?)

When you're in your early teens everything in you is changing its shape and changing its mind. You want to rebel, you want to heartily disagree with anything anyone says, and because of your friends, you don't want to like what anyone over the age of eighteen likes. Even if you love something to death, once you find an adult that likes it too, you might as well tear it up and throw it away. Can you imagine anything a awful as fancying the same bloke as your aunt? ('Ooh, isn't that nice Jason Donovan lovely?')

Worse still is when someone of sixteen years old discovers you like something that they don't. ('Oh come on! You can't *possibly* fancy him!')

It's a bewildering world, the world of a thirteen-year-old. How on earth are they supposed to know who to look up to, who to follow and who's right and wrong? Everyone around them seems to know what's best and nobody's telling them why.

The majority of people in the world can't talk to a young teen. Although this isn't a fact that's been proven, John and I have talked to very few people who have made us think otherwise. And here we will let you into a rather horrible secret. The

45

majority of people in the world *don't want to talk to young teens*! This is ridiculously sad but true. Our timetable is nearly always full through lack of other youth workers who won't take on The Brat Pack. For some strange reason *there appears to be a stigma attached to this age-group*. If you put a hundred youth leaders in a room and told them they had a choice between working with over-sixteens or under-sixteens, we could almost guarantee that, when expressing a preference, eight out of ten youth leaders prefer working with older teens – and that's being very generous!

WHY ARE YOUNG TEENS SO DIFFICULT?

So, I think we can draw a swift conclusion here. But the question is why? Why doesn't anyone want to work with them? Well, I think one reason is that it's not so much that people don't want to work with this age, as the fact that they really don't know how to talk to them. So here's a tip. *Don't treat them too young*. If you talk to them like little kids, that's what you'll end up with – little kids. They will muck about and become silly, hitting each other and shouting above you all the time. If on the other hand you treat them like little adults . . . that's how they'll respond!

WHAT? WHY? WHERE? . . . THEY CAN REASON

We love doing debates with this age-group. Sometimes we don't give kids enough credit for the reasoning that goes on inside their minds.

On a number of occasions, we have had some pretty hot discussions going on all sorts of issues. Relationships . . . War and Peace . . . Law and order . . . School . . . Parents. Now, if you just sat down and tried to discuss these issues generally with them, you might find that they all clam up on you. It's no good saying to kids of this age; 'What do you think of war?' and expecting them to come up with a five-page essay answer. Their most likely answers will be 'Dunno', 'S'all right', or 'Boring'. On the other hand, if you treat them as if you actually care about their answers then things will become very different indeed. Your approach is vital.

This is the way we do it:

Let's take the subject of school. OK, we are going to discuss the problems of school from a Christian standpoint, so first of all we need one or two Christian teachers to take part. They can be from different schools. Then we need at least one teacher who is not a Christian. These three people will form a sort of panel and will sit behind a table on a stage, or at least in front of the kids. Next we need someone to put in the 'Hot Spot' . . . maybe someone of a different standing, like a school governor, or someone from the P.T.A. This person sits or stands in the middle of the stage with you (or the appropriate youth leader). Now, we need one of the most important ingredients – a panel of brats! Three or four kids who are willing to be outspoken, to sit behind a table on the opposite side of the stage to the teachers.

Already we have a recipe for all-out war!

By the way, the reasoning behind the tables, is that you give your panels plenty of pens and doodling paper for them to write down things they want to say, should they get half a chance! You now have your stage set for an interesting debate. The only thing that is missing is the important part your 'audience' will play. They are not there to sit still and listen, they are there to agree, disagree, shout and heckle.

Be professional. Because of this, you will find yourself needing a microphone on a very long lead that can reach out to where they are. Now we are set!

The idea of a debate is to pull an argument from both sides, and to get this going you need to ask some fairly outrageous questions (e.g. 'Is killing another human ever right?' or maybe 'Should caning be brought back to schools?'), so make sure that your guests realize that they are in for a fairly rough ride, and that because this is basically a young teens meeting . . . things shouldn't be taken any further than that meeting, unless there's a jolly good reason.

There are plenty of moral issues to throw around, and we've found that one of the things that drives kids mad at school is 'confiscation'. Strong feelings generate good reaction, so if you want to start with a real wind-up, talk about that.

Get the audience involved. Go to them first and ask them if they've ever had something confiscated and how long for. Plenty of kids will put their hands up for this. Then ask them if they know what happened to their belongings during that confiscation time. This is when you will find out, to your dismay, that some of the kids know for a fact that their toys have been taken home by the teachers and used by their own children. You will probably also find out that their magazines have been passed round the staffroom.

By now, your panels will be dying to plead their case . . . so when they have had their say, remember to go to the panel of kids for some statements.

Most of the time, the debate will run itself from here, but *it's worth having plenty of questions and subjects ready*, in case it dries up. The moral issues in school can cause quite a commotion, but it also gives the teachers a chance to explain why things happen the way they do, why detention can be a good thing and how they see the homework load. You can talk about 'grassing' on fellow pupils – when should you say something and when should you keep quiet? If your teacher disagrees with your Christian viewpoint, should you challenge him or let it go? Really, it's endless, and you will see your young teens acting in a very grown up way as they try to explain how they feel – maybe for the first time.

Gaining an insight into your youth group

This kind of debate will give you a huge insight into the kids in your group, and once you are aware of how they think and feel, you'll be much more able to talk to them and understand why they say the things they do.

On the other hand if you are having a night when you want to talk about a particular subject and you have no 'professional people' to call on, there are other ways.

ANOTHER APPROACH – 'THE BIN'

One that we have found particularly successful, is the use of a bin and some paper and pens. First of all, you could chat for a while about the subject – again throwing out outrageous comments to help the kids have something to come back on.

Recently, we took a load of fifteen-year-old pupils on the subjects of sex, marriage and divorce. We were in school time and these subjects are catered for under P.S.E. (Personal and Social Education). We were asked to put forward our views as Christians and as a married couple. The first thing we asked was 'Why isn't "love" included in the title of the lesson?' We went on to expound on the fact that our marriage was built around the fact that we were very much in love . . . in fact John proposed after just a week of going out with me. We talked about 'love at first sight' and 'someone who is especially made for you' . . . as well as the more common subjects of sex before marriage, etc.

Now, this is where the bin comes in. After we've spoken for a while, we gear the kids up to ask us questions and rather than getting them to vocalize, we ask them to write their questions down. We share out pens and paper and tell them that we would like their questions to be anonymous, so that instead of asking what you think you *should ask*, you actually ask what you really wanted to ask. This works incredibly well, and although we first thought we would get loads of silly questions, we got very few. And the amazing thing with this particular topic was that the questions that the kids really wanted to ask were totally different from the ones we expected. In every case, by far the most popular question is always 'How do I know when I've met the right one?' This question outweighs the others by about three to one.

We tend to go around the group with our bin and ask the kids to fold the paper up and put it in the bin. *It helps for you to physically go round with the bin*, because kids haven't got the confidence to walk up to the front and drop the question in themselves.

Remember to keep adult and professional in your approach.

Please try and help when you can and don't resort to saying stupid things like 'Come on! You're old enough to do this for yourself.' Most subjects that young teens want to talk about are embarrassing to them, or very close to their hearts and *putting them down will only ever result in them either clamming up, or doing things 'because you asked them'* and not because they wanted to.

After we have a fair few questions in the bin, we begin to sort them out. This gives other kids time to write more and it gives you time to sift through and find out what the main questions are. When we start to read them out to the kids, we take it seriously and answer as honestly as we can. There are times when humour obviously comes into it, but again it has to be genuine and not some jocular remark about a 'silly teenage problem'.

THE PERSON BEHIND THE 'FRONT'

After one particular lesson like this, two teachers came up to us with a screwed-up piece of paper and said, 'We thought you might like to see this.' Then they explained that it had been found on the desk of a girl who'd been very loud and outspoken during the lesson, and they recognized her handwriting. The note said, 'You can tell they're in love by the way she looks at him.'

Both the teachers were quite bemused by this, because they would never have thought of such a girl even entertaining such soppy thoughts! So there you are – the outside of most teenagers is a cover – a much-needed cover, but a cover just the same. *Don't be put off by what they say to you, but try different ways to find out what they really mean.*

The bin can be used in a variety of ways. It's proved very popular for us and as we've said before in this book, it's easier for kids to write their feelings down than stand up and tell the world . . . but treat them right and they'll start to trust you.

As I'm typing this, we've been working in a particularly awkward school, where the teenagers are suspicious of your motives as soon as you walk through the door. It's taken us about four days to gain their trust, but now they are waving at us in the street and sitting with us while we eat our lunch. We've done our best to treat them with respect and not to close in on their space and we're now being rewarded for it.

And in one way it's easy to tell when you've treated 'em right. They've been coming up all day saying:

'Would you like me to fix the lights for the concert? I'll come in after school.'

'Can we help you carry your things to the car?'

'Shall I see if I can get you a drink from the office?'

'What do you think I should wear tonight?'

'Can I bring my friends to your concert?'

'I know this bloke . . . he's a Christian like you.'

So, when they start offering to make the coffee and asking advice . . . you've cracked it!

SUMMARY

Remember being awkward can be the result of the many changes, emotional and physical, that they are going through.

Never talk down to them or belittle them.

Encourage their natural inquisitiveness.

There is more to a person than the 'front' you see.

Right Place, Right Time . . . Right Calling?

WHY oh why did you become a youth leader? It's a question every worker asks himself every Friday night. In a recent youth leaders' seminar we were leading, many of the adults there confessed that it was a case of 'There was no-one else to do it.'

Availability

Most youth leaders do not feel 'qualified' for the position they are in and think they are floundering around in deep water. The strange thing is that so many of them come to youth leaders' training days and the like, which only leads us to believe one thing – they actually want to make a go of it. Maybe in the first instance it was a case of there being no-one else available, but happily a lot of you have seen the plight of our youngsters and have taken it on board regardless. So this chapter is especially for you and about you, and we hope it will help you to grow.

We are going to look at several aspects of the life and work of the youth leader, to try and put it all into perspective. First of all we have:

The Organizer

A great deal of your time will be taken up organizing events and trips out, booking people to come and speak to your kids, and just generally making sure the tuck shop is full. This is a very important part of your job, basically because the kids you are overseeing are really too young to be doing much of it for themselves. They might be able to come up with a great idea for a night out, but that's where it ends. *Getting it actually to happen is your job.* Don't expect too much of your crowd, they are indecisive and just haven't the confidence to make much of a decision when it comes to things like 'Do you want to go Wednesday or Friday?' or 'Do you want to go ice-skating or tenpin bowling?' They don't know. Take the initiative – you are the leader! They want *you* to tell them! If you say 'We are going bowling on Friday night, be here at seven thirty' there's a good chance they will just turn up, whereas if you specifically ask them if they can make it, you'll get the 'don't knows' again. They also want picking up in the minibus and taking there and back!

We know a great guy in Birmingham who organizes loads of events for his youth group. He's a very ordinary bloke and very unassuming. He's not trendy, he's not young but he's a good organizer. He'll say to them 'Now, in a month's time we are going to EuroDisney, so you've got twenty-eight days to save up all your money.' He doesn't ask them, he just informs them and straight away there are questions. 'How much?' 'Are we going by coach?' 'Is it just for us or can my friends come?' It's wonderful to watch and I'm sure he hasn't a clue why they react this way to him. He just *treats them right* and he's not afraid to put himself up for a laugh. He'll say: 'I'll buy a hot dog for the first person who can manage to get me on one of those awful rides!' He's not trying to be 'one of the lads'. He's trying to be the youth leader who's treating his kids to a great day out. He takes the weight of all the organizing and the kids have all the fun, and that's the way it should be. If you are fortunate enough to have more than one youth leader on your team, then you can *share the load* – but, as we've said before, filling in the forms and buying the tickets is your problem!

YOU ARE THE EXAMPLE . . . Yes it makes you tremble a bit, doesn't it? Like it or lump it, you are your youth group's role model!!

You are most likely to be the only proper Christian that the kids have got to go on. They will look to you for guidance, and will watch to see how you react to things, how you cope with life.

John and I set ourselves up for this kind of grilling nearly every day of our lives. We are under close scrutiny from teenagers in schools every week, just waiting to see if we will lose our tempers, how far they can push us and wanting to see the Christian mask crack! When we used to play in pubs, we were often sent a tray of beers by appreciative groups of people. As it happens neither John nor I drink much, and neither of us likes beer, so we usually asked if the barman would take them back and send some Cokes instead. Now, although sometimes the people would say, 'Go on! Have a drink, you've deserved it!' We knew that if we downed a pint, then someone would be waiting to say, 'See! They are just like us!' Now I'm not saying drinking is wrong, it's just that in those circumstances you are influencing a lot of lives and people don't want you to be 'the same as them' . . . they are looking for something different. And it's the same with your youth group, they may say you are old-fashioned but, believe me, they wouldn't want you any other way. *They need your example as a Christian*, because they may not have such an example at home. Where there are no Christian parents to set the scene, they need someone to measure up again, a trusted example outside the family. And sometimes, what your parents say is going to get up your nose anyway, Christian or no, because you need someone outside of your home to be an influence to you. I know that my sister went through a stage of wearing those fishnet stockings and my mum really didn't like them. She tried everything to stop her wearing them but, of course, it only made her want to wear them more! Then one day, a lady at work told my sister that her stockings didn't look very nice . . . and she never wore them again! Ever! We tend to think our family have some kind of ulterior motive because they know us through and through, whereas if someone outside the family says it, then it must be true!

Your youth group know that you have authority and you care about them – the same as their family – but you are not overall responsible for them and you don't run their lives on a day-to-day basis, so they are more willing to listen to you and watch what you do and respect it.

I always think it was terrific that Paul could say, 'Be imitators of me, as I imitate Christ' (1 Corinthians 11:1). I don't think it's at all big-headed to say that, it's just totally confident – and *that's what kids need to see – your total confidence in the Lord!*

The Enthuser

You've probably noticed that everything in the life of your youth group is 'boring' . . . well, believe it or not, you are the one that can change their thinking. If you have enthusiasm for something, then they will gradually follow suit. You know what it's like at home when the lawn needs mowing, if you have no enthusiasm for the job it takes for ever. John is always saying that. He looks out over the grass and thinks 'I really don't want to do this. It's a boring job and I hate it. It's only going to grow again anyway.' With this kind of attitude, it takes John a million years to cut the grass. On the other hand, some days he will look at the sunshine and say to me, 'You know, I think I'll have a go at that lawn.' It's done within minutes! Really it is, you ask him!

ENJOY WHAT YOU ARE DOING . . .

We have to have the same attitude for our youth meetings. There is no way any kid is going to enjoy *anything* if you walk in looking like a wet weekend.

There's something about an unenthusiastic person that completely finishes a youth group. I can remember going to a youth meeting where everyone was sitting round in a circle and looking at this bloke who was supposed to be leading them. He just sort of sat there, looking at the floor and gradually twiddled his fingers before he summoned up the energy to mumble: 'So, what shall we do tonight?' It was pitiful and completely frustrating and I remember quite vividly taking the poor bloke to task on it. I just couldn't sit there any longer and watch him die of boredom and take everyone else with him . . . It was time for drastic action, so I really wiped the floor with him! As much as I felt sorry for him, he wouldn't let go of the job of youth leader because it gave him a 'position' in the church! This is just not on! The next week he came into the meeting a much brighter, cheerful fella . . . still dull, but much brighter . . . and he'd actually worked out a programme beforehand so that he could encourage everyone to join in.

It doesn't matter which way you look at youth work, *you simply must have a really good reason for heading it up*. If you like kids and want to help – if you are an active person who can teach kids – if you are simply a parent who recognizes his kids' needs . . . then these are all good reasons and your enthusiasm for the job will shine through.

The Risk-Taker

The one who enables. When talking about risks, we don't mean so much the guy who will take the kids mountain climbing, as the person who will stick his neck out when things could go drastically wrong.

Take the church service, for instance. Organizing your group to take the morning service can be a huge headache. What if it goes wrong? They don't turn up? They forget what to do? Yes, it's all going to come back to you! The risk-taker. Somewhere along the line, your youth group have to learn and experience things for themselves, and taking the service is one way they grow. Of course they are going to do it wrong, but if your congregation are concerned for today's youth, then they will manage to swallow the few dodgy guitar chords and sketch that doesn't quite come off.

Can you remember giving your testimony for the first time? Lousy, wasn't it? You stumbled over the easy bits and couldn't remember the vital point you were trying to make and then you left out the most important bit – even though you had it all written out on that sweaty bit of paper. So, come on, how many people came up to you afterwards and said, 'Well, you didn't do very well, did you? Why couldn't you stop shaking and let your voice calm down a bit?'

Nobody. More than anything, I'm sure you had people saying 'Well done! That was terrific! It's good to know a little bit more about your life.'

Happily, taking part in the service is not part of some serious oral exam. People should not be judging your performance and holding up cards at the end to give you some kind of score! Part of your job as an encourager is to give people the opportunity to grow as Christians, and as the risk-taker you need to stand beside them smiling, while they carve it up.

GIVE KIDS AN OPPORTUNITY TO GROW.

We were at a church once where some of the young people were going to sing a song in the service. They came to the front, put on guitars and stood in a long row of about five or six. Then instead of counting themselves in, or one of them playing an introduction to the song, the guy on the end looked at the rest of the group and shouted 'Go!' And then they all played furiously in whatever rhythm or key they happened to fancy! It was quite incredible to watch, and I'm sure they learnt a lot from the experience. You see, people improve. Especially kids, because they are at the learning period of their lives. They catch on very quickly, and very soon they become confident and good at their particular gifts.

A minister we know up north had a daughter who was desperate to form a worship band in the church and it was causing all sorts of headaches for the minister. This was mainly because he had heard them practise and he knew it was going to be hard work for his congregation and, as his own daughter was involved, he felt that it was all going to land on his shoulders. He was right, of course, but we persuaded him to let them play, maybe once a month for special services, and so he became the risk-taker. Eventually the worship band got it together and now they are really good, but somewhere along the line, someone had to put their head on the block. As a youth leader, it has to be your head. Your kids need to be part of what's happening now not when they have achieved greatness by going to university and getting a music degree!!

PART TWO

God's Calling

We thought we should split this chapter up because, as well as talking about your position as a youth leader, we also wanted to talk more personally about you as a Christian. We all spend time standing around asking the Lord to tell us in words of one syllable, what it is He wants us to do for Him. Most of the time we don't listen to the answer – but we do so love asking the question! It's a bit like putting your hand into a 'lucky dip' and not getting what you hoped for, so you try again. You know that somewhere in that bag is the thing you would really like, and if you keep trying you will pull it out and then you can shout out, 'Hey! Wasn't that lucky!' . . . as if it was your first attempt. The thing we have to try to get through our heads is that *God actually wants us to be happy!* That 'thing' that we would love to do is quite probably the very thing the Lord wants us to do . . . but we don't listen. Why didn't we just search through the bag and pull out the prize in the first place??

WHAT DOES GOD WANT OF ME?

It is very important that you know for certain that the Lord wants you to serve Him in a specific way. And there is only one way to find out if it's for you, and that's to give it a shot!

Now, maybe that doesn't sound very spiritual, but you have to take steps to find out where you belong   you can't expect God to keep waggling your legs for you. If you fall over badly . . . it's probably not for you.

We have listed the kinds of attributes that will help you in your work as a youth leader and we have also pointed out the fact that a lot of unlikely people make the best leaders. The ultimate point is: *Does the Lord want you to do it?* If he does, then you will survive in the face of moans and groans . . . moans from the kids, and groans from the rest of the church who are put off by the enthusiastic yells of the kids who moaned at you in the first place! It is important to know that God is cheering you on and you are in the right place with Him.

You won't survive for very long if you are trying to do this work on your own. Listen to these wise words from one John Ritter: 'At times you will want to pack it in and the only reason you will keep doing it is because the Lord has asked you. To stop doing it would be to disobey Him.' Strong words, but true. If you find yourself in this predicament, then you know you are in the right place with God, and everything's going along fine!

CAN I COPE?

Serving the Lord was never meant to be an easy option, but the Lord knows that you can actually cope with the stress and strain of youth work – otherwise he wouldn't ask you to do it. Sometimes the Lord says to John and me: 'I am going to stretch you.' They are not our most favourite words, but they are words that, we have to admit, the Lord seems to favour using when wanting to make a point with us. We will be asked to do something that we honestly don't think we can cope with or that we actually *know we can't do!* – but somehow we find ourselves nodding and saying okay, and somehow we find the strength or wisdom to do it . . . We've had to write a theme song with two days' notice (we couldn't do that) . . . we've had to take five seminars because someone was ill and went home (we couldn't do that) . . . we've had to act out five different parts for a video (we definitely couldn't do that!) . . . and we've had to hold a roadshow together for five hours because it was raining outside (no chance!). But each time, the Lord said: 'Sorry this might hurt a bit, but it's stretching time again!'

God knows that you can cope with the hassles otherwise He would never ask you to do it. Youth work is the ultimate hassle, so you need to make sure you have your reasons and your calling round the right way to begin with. The right place at the right time, eh?

The Family
Yes! Remember them?? Those people you used to have time for before you were called into working with young people! 'Time' is the important word here. Having lectured you on giving yourselves wholeheartedly to your youth group, we now need to make sure you don't neglect your family.

YOUR FIRST PRIORITY

Your family must always come before your youth work; it is vital that you don't ignore or abuse time with them. It's going to be like juggling plates on the ends of long sticks, but your youth group should not be an extension of your own loved ones. It is good to have them all round to your house, and to have them mix with the rest of your tribe, but you must also be very careful that they don't take over. Be overcautious with your husband or wife when inviting the gang round. Make sure it's a good time for everyone, and not when your own kids are trying to study for exams . . . or when they are out.

INCLUDE YOUR OWN KIDS. Maybe your own kids don't like going to church, but they might get something out of having a youth meeting round at the house, so don't cut them off; make sure they are included. Don't hold the church kids up against your own kids. Saying things like 'Don't you wish you had a testimony like Darren's?' is not a good idea. Your own family are most precious . . . and you know that. If you look around you, you will see families dropping like flies, being torn apart for no end of reasons . . . and unhappily we have seen families wrecked by the overenthusiastic youth leader.

FAMILY TIME IS VITAL. Driving your family crazy with constant references to the youth group, visits to your house eight days a week and no time for your own kids, is not good for you, it's not good for them . . . and it's of no value to the youth group.

There is no secret formula to the youth leader game, there is no particular image to conform to. The youth worker is all types of men and women . . .

Getting the balance right is of prime importance here, because we want God to use you, stretch you and be proud of you!

SUMMARY

Be available to God each day.

An organizer, example, friend, enthuser – you may not be all these people, but you should be some.

Enjoy what you do . . . it will keep you sane!

Take risks – stretch yourself.

Give opportunity to your youth group. Stretch them, they are pliable.

Do what the Lord asks with all your strength.

Keep tabs on your time – your first calling is to your family.

CHAPTER TEN

God Uses Kids All the Time!

P ERSONALLY, I think God loves using brats! Why shouldn't he? They are bolshie, brash, exciting and they don't care how far they stick their necks out if they believe that what they are doing is right.

ENTHUSIASM, BUT LACKING WISDOM

Of course, you *do* have to be fairly sure that it's God who's using them, and not their egos! A while ago we were just about to take a school assembly. We had set up our thousand-watt P.A. in the school hall and were waiting for the headmaster to announce us to the 500 or so pupils waiting to hear us. And then, just as we were about to start our first song, this fourth-former came running onto the stage. Not knowing what was happening, (and not being known for my finesse . . .) I stopped him with my boot and asked him what on earth he thought he was doing. He gave me a very pious look and told me he had a message from the Lord for the school. Now, I knew immediately that this guy was wrong. It was all very nice that he was a Christian, and he'd seen us going down well in the school, but this was definitely not the time to give a word of prophecy. So I told him he would have to go and sit down and talk to us afterwards, but he wouldn't go! He wanted a piece of the action! What he didn't understand was that he could have easily closed the school from having another visit from Christians ever again. Finally my boot managed to persuade him that perhaps it would be as well if he disappeared for the time being and we did see him afterwards to explain the situation.

Even so, I would rather that he tried than not! Wouldn't it be great if all our young Christians were so zealous in their faith that we had to keep kicking them away from the front of the church!!

The great thing about the Brat Pack age is that they have no *inhibitions*. So although this kid was wrong he still did it!

PRAYER WITHOUT THE JARGON

It's a marvellous thing to hear kids pray. I try really hard to keep my prayers simple in order to encourage their own. If we can pray 'Lord, I've had a really naff day at work, so it's good to come and have a chat with you. My friend said he doesn't think you're doing a very good job, but I didn't mind because it gave me a chance to talk to him about you, so Lord shake him up a bit for me, will you? Amen.' *Then*, you will find that the kids in your youth group will follow suit.

We did a youth weekend with around fifty kids and part of the fun thing we were doing was to stamp people's foreheads with a rubber stamp with YO! on it. It became a most wanted item. Everyone wanted YO! on their forehead! The one of the leaders asked what it meant. So we said that it was just a modern term for agreeing with someone. A way of saying: 'Yes, you're right! I agree! I feel the same way! . . . oh all right then . . . Amen.' So after this, we advised the kids to end their prayers with the word YO! It was brilliant! People wanted to pray, just so they could say YO! at the end, but gradually it became a more definite YO! When we came back to the church after the weekend, we attended the Sunday night service and when the minister prayed there was a huge heartfelt YO! at the end of his prayer. It was great! The rest of the congregation were greatly amused . . . they'd never heard their young people so vocal before!

FAITH AS A TEENAGER

When kids pray and really mean it, they don't pray things like 'if it's your will'. They just get on and pray. I mean, they have no concept of God *not* answering their prayers. They put their faith totally on the line and because of that they see results. We've seen loads of kids pray for the sick, and not for a minute have they even considered unanswered prayer. We were in a situation once where young people were coming to the front of a meeting for healing and the guy that was praying for them was happily doing his stuff, and then afterwards a few girls came up to him and said: 'Would you pray for our friend's hand?' The girl in question lifted up a hand that had no fingers. Now, this wasn't a problem for the young girls, but it was a problem for the speaker.

We saw him afterwards and he admitted that he just hadn't got the faith to pray for that little girl. 'I just didn't know what to say,' he said sadly. 'I made up some pathetic excuse about being busy and seeing her later.'

That evening the girls came back to him smiling and his stomach turned over. They walked up to him and said: 'Oh you don't have to pray for our friend now, we prayed for her this afternoon and we think that the bumps on her hand are growing.'

It was no big deal. Their only concern was just to tell the guy that he had one less problem to sort out. I don't know how she is today, because I only saw her once, but their faith was a lesson to much more mature Christians!

The Bible, of course, is full of kids who walked out in faith because they knew God wanted them to. I don't know, maybe as you get older and more experienced in 'life', it actually throws stumbling blocks in your way. We see the arguments, the sensible reasons for *not* doing that God asks of us. We reason, and put forward really wonderful excuses, we start getting realistic and 'adult' about it all. Perhaps there's a case there for us acting more like brats at times.

AN INSPIRATIONAL CHARACTER – FAITH IN SPITE OF CIRCUMSTANCES

Take a look at Joseph. A totally inspirational character and thanks to Tim Rice and Andrew Lloyd Webber he's more popular today than he's ever been! Joseph was only a brat when God started giving him dreams. He started showing Joseph the story of his life through pictures of corn sheaves bowing down to lesser sheaves. A teenager being worshipped by his family? But *Joseph wasn't going to let go of his dream just because it was absurd!* No way! God gave him that vision and not only was he going to hold on to it but he was going to tell anyone who wanted to listen! So, when his brothers got more than a little annoyed with him, he shrugged it off and carried on believing. Then – when his brothers had finally had enough of this little brat and his holier-than-thou attitude – they sold him to some passing Ishmaelites and thought they'd never near of him again.

When Joseph had been beaten up, betrayed and put into jail, you tend to think he would have started to wonder if either the whole thing had been in his imagination or his interpretation of what God was trying to say was wrong. But Joseph was one of The Brat Pack . . . he didn't give up just because things weren't going his way. He firmly believed that God had spoken to him and that come hell or high water he was going to be some kind of ruler! He wasn't swayed at all by his circumstances. God said it and Joseph believed it – what was so complicated about that? And of course he was right. God did make him into a ruler, he saved his own family and the whole of Caanan from starvation.

FAITH IN SPITE OF WELL-INFORMED OPPOSITION

Another character who started life out as a brat, was David. The little kid who looked after the sheep while all his brothers went to play war games. David was curious. He knew that his brothers were in the battle line and he wanted to see the army with God on their side, doing their stuff. So when he was asked to take some sandwiches down to the front line, he was dead chuffed. This was his chance to see the God in whom he believed 100% – in action! It was going to be terrific! God was going to show this load of Philistines what for, and David was going to swell with pride as he saw his brothers attack and win the fight.

So what a letdown it must have been to walk into the scene of Goliath shouting his head off at everyone, and the army of God trembling at the sight of him.

You see, for a brat it was inconceivable that people could possibly be scared when God had already told you it was going to be all right.

The wonderful thing about the story of David and Goliath is that David was prepared for anything. He didn't come down to the battle prepared to fight, or prepared to serve his brothers . . . he came prepared for anything. *Anything* that God wanted to do was all right by him. So, once he'd been told the full story of the fact that whoever fought the giant won the battle, he couldn't understand why no-one wanted to fight him. 'But we are the army of God, and he's some uncircumcised Philistine! What's the problem?'

The retort from his brothers and the rest of the army was that he should push off back to his sheep and stop waving his arms about. But David was totally insistent that someone should be fighting this Goliath person. So he volunteeered. Kids today get the same informed reaction – what a discouragement! And that's where we get all the comments that kids still get thrown at them now . . .

'Don't be so stupid!'

'You're much too young!'

'You don't understand!'

'You're too small and the armour won't fit!'

'Go away and let the adults handle it.'

Things haven't changed that much, have they? But happily, David wasn't having any of it. Who needed armour? What had age got to do with it? God was on his side . . . it was all so simple! And as we know, David killed Goliath with a stone. It just didn't occur to him that maybe it was dangerous, because he knew that God was on his side!

God uses brats more and more because they are fearless in the face of danger, because they don't care about the armour and they don't realize that having the wrong accent or coming from the 'wrong part of town' is a major problem!

I hope that makes you ache for the days when *you* felt like that!

Teens have to handle many difficulties we never had to face.

Young Christian kids don't get the credit they deserve half the time. Mainly because they would never dream of telling you about half the scrapes they get into. The reason behind this is that they don't like to 'grass' on their friends. John and I have been in situations where kids have been very straight with us and told us of escapades in their lives that would make their parents' hair stand on end.

I can remember one girl who told us about a certain situation in her church. She hadn't come to us to tell a story, we were just talking about something else and she obviously felt she should say something. Apparently, after a Sunday night service it had become the 'in' thing to do to go down to a piece of waste land away from the church, and here they had their own 'meeting'.

There was a small opening somewhat like a small cave that they met in, and the idea was that they put a curtain up halfway and took it in turns to go behind the curtain in couples. The young girl refused to be part of it and after a few weeks she actually stood up in front of them all and told them exactly what she thought of them. Bearing in mind that she was only fifteen years old, I think she deserved a medal! Single-handedly she destroyed a real 'den of iniquity' and got them back on the right road . . . but nobody else knew about this. She wasn't after any acclaim, she just knew what God liked and disliked.

The same went for a young boy who at the age of fourteen told us how he regularly went to a secret place with his school-friends on the school premises, while they smoked pot. He said to us with wide eyes: 'I just stand with them. I've told them I think it's stupid and I won't join in, so I just stand back while they get on with it. But they're my friends, so I go with them.' When you are fourteen, you don't consider the law as much as you consider your friends. And we were quite stunned that this boy could quietly go about his own life while having to stand as a Christian in extremely difficult situations. But once again, the Brat Mentality says: 'I know what's right and wrong, so I'll make my stand.'

Salt and Light

Christians are supposed to be 'salt and light' in a world that's rotting. Unfortunately, many of us prefer to take the *easy way out* and *withdraw* from a situation rather than make a *difference* to it. Kids stand up much more because either they are unaware of danger or don't worry so much about the conse-quences. I often wonder what 'loud adult Christians' are like at work, don't you? You see them at the meetings waving their fists and praying at a volume that would set off alarms. Perhaps they are like that in the office . . . somehow I doubt it. When I first became a Christian I was very excited and told people that I worked with, and it was only then that I found out that there were other Christians in the building and work-based acquaintances that were Christians too. I had quite a field day introducing them all to each other and gradually pulling them together! No-one was safe any more, and the fact that I worked with 'pop stars' and famous people meant that the gossip it caused was all the more fun!

It's a fact that the longer you leave it to tell someone about your faith, the harder it gets, and maybe that's why kids stand up for Jesus so much more, because they are relatively new Christians. As you get older in the faith, change jobs, etc., you find it harder to talk about it. I know quite a few Christian teachers who can discuss any issue with their pupils, but can't relate Christianity to them.

Interesting, isn't it? If you put yourself beside some Christian brats that you know . . . how do you measure up??

SUMMARY

Youth have enthusiasm and need your wisdom to steer, not dampen it.

Be a modern example of how to pray.

Keep faith simple.

Encourage their initiative – however risky.

It takes courage to stand in front of 1,000 kids at school and say, 'I am a Christian.'

Make a difference as salt and light.

Fancy That!

THE Brat Pack age has got to be the very worst age for the dating game. Everything surrounding it is new, and nobody knows what to do about it. It's a time where rumours are rife . . . even in this day and age when we think that kids know the facts of life backwards. In fact, that's some of the problem really . . . they get some of it backwards!

RIGHT INFORMATION . . . BUT NO GUIDELINES

They are fed with so much information at such an early age, learning things that should be of no relevance to them at this stage.

John and I went into a classroom in a 'middle school' where the kids were nine- to thirteen-year-olds and were very surprised to find a 'test' on the blackboard asking questions like: 'Name three reasons why boys prefer not to use condoms.' When the questions get to this level, then it's no wonder that kids get confused.

THE RELATIONSHIP PRESSURES

Wouldn't it be great if someone gave them some advice on how to ask their first date out? Or what to say when you go out with him or her? Let's face it, most kids have problems with these things! Going on your first date can be an horrendous experience, and if a young boy listens to the advice of his friends – he's doomed for ever. Well, in reality they've probably never been out with anyone either! There is a pressure, once you are in your teens, to be able to say that you have a girlfriend or boyfriend. This always leads to about 75% of all kids telling lies, because it's the only way round this issue. No-one wants to be thought of as being the only person not going out with someone, so relationships get fabricated. This again leads to all sorts of disasters; I well remember myself and a friend inventing two boys, just to shut the rest of our gang up for a while. We spent time thinking up good names for them, and of course they came from 'another school, you wouldn't know them'. Our friends became suspicious and started to separate us and ask us all sorts of questions, so then we had to think of a 'double date' that we'd been on. We looked up a review of a film that was on locally and tried to rehearse what the film was like and everything. It was so stupid, because when we got stuck on questions about the plot of the film, we innocently explained that we hadn't been concentrating and didn't see all of it. Unfortunately, by the time the story got round our class, my friend and I were reputationless! And none of it was true, there wasn't even a boyfriend! . . . At least we weren't as bad as the girls that were caught giving themselves lovebites in the loo!

But it's awful, the pressure to go out with someone before you're ready for it is quite crazy. People get so hurt too, thinking that someone really likes them, when in the end it was all done for a bet. Anyway, let's look more closely at different aspects of relationships.

GIRLS VERSUS GOD

Still one of the best comments we've ever had on this subject came from two girls who came to us in great anguish over their Christian lives. The problem, it turned out, was that, if they were honest, they found teenage boys more attractive than God.

I can remember my heart going out to them, they were so serious and almost tearful because they so much wanted to do the right thing as Christians . . . but just lately this problem was becoming enormous. I asked them how old they were and they replied 'Fourteen.' Now, I know I'm always telling you not to mock teenagers . . . but this was one time when I laughed. They looked very surprised and most distressed. Then I explained that fourteen-year-old girls were *supposed* to have their heads turned by boys! That's the way God planned it! It's part of life, it's great fun and above all, very natural! Boys have been turning girls' heads and vice versa since time began!

By now they looked even more astonished. Yes, of course God should be number one – but there's certainly room enough in your life for other things. They were both so relieved to find out that they were not abnormal in any way, and we prayed with them and they prayed too and realized that God had not removed himself from them because their eyes strayed during the sermon!

MY FRIEND FANCIES YOU!

The 'fancying each other' bit is the largest part of their lives at this time and as we have talked about with other subjects, this one is often dealt with by means of written communication. There is a process, that usually begins with the boy asking his friend to ask one of her friends if she likes him. This is then followed by one of her friends telling one of his friends that this is true. Now we have a situation where they both know they like each other, but neither are prepared to do anything about it! So it's time to start writing notes! Letter writing can go on for weeks on end, notes get passed in classes, assemblies, break times and still no-one is any nearer going out with anyone.

IT'S FUN, BUT IT'S IMPORTANT TO THEM

At our concerts, one of the favourite things the kids love is that we put a red bin on the front of the stage and surround it with hundreds of bits of scrap paper and pens. We get the kids to write to us and we read the letters out in between our songs. We ask them to tell us their favourite jokes, requests for songs and, of course, who fancies who. The storm towards the bin is amazing to watch, there are bits of paper flying everywhere and fights going on to secure a pen. Anyone who has been to one of our concerts will tell you about this phenomenon!

It's a fantastic attention holder. You can tell them anything, sing them anything, just as long as you have a pile of letters on the top of your keyboard, waiting to be read out. They scream and shout at us all the way through the concert, so concerned that *the one* of all time won't get read out! It's so important to them. I was chatting to a guy this week who could remember us going to his school three years ago and he could still quote the letters that we read out about him! *We must not neglect the magnitude of importance a kid attaches to a letter.*

INEXPRESSIBLE FEELINGS

They are too young to speak for themselves, so a note has to say it all, and really when you understand that they are too tongue-tied to ask someone out, you can also see that an awful lot of them are just too young to be getting involved.

They go to great lengths to get noticed by the opposite sex. Girls tend to giggle extremely loudly and nudge their friends. They find it immensely funny to shout the names of their friends out loud, (just in case the boy doesn't know what her name is . . .) or hang around casually outside his house. And they believe, they really believe, that the boy in question has no idea that this is part of their 'plan'. If you ever say to a thirteen-year-old girl, 'You like him, don't you?' She will look at you in utter amazement and say, 'How did you know?'

Boys, on the other hand, like to fight each other.

If they like a girl, the chances are they will spar with their partners every time she appears. They will skateboard up and down the place where she stands, or they'll pose on their bikes. Again, they don't seem to realize that every adult has read the signs a hundred times before, and knows exactly what's going on, it's only the girl wishing they'd stop fighting that doesn't realize it's all being done for her benefit!

But, you see, they just don't have the words. That's what it's all about. Young teens are not talkative, and it's not because they don't like you, it's because they are terribly scared of saying the wrong thing and looking a complete idiot. We need to give them space, and when it comes to relationships we need to help not hinder. It's painful . . . don't you remember?'

LET'S GET PHYSICAL?

John and I don't want to turn this chapter into a sex manual, as we feel that *that* is a book in itself, so although it may look as if we are glossing over the issue, we don't want it to appear flippant. Kids need to talk about sex, and they need to have the basics put over in a way that they can understand. When we take Personal and Social Education lessons in schools, we find that young people are still far more interested in the mystery of love, than they are in the physical side of a relationship. They've seen all the movies, heard the crude jokes and discussed rape and abortion until it would make your head spin . . . but hardly anyone talks to them about love.

LOVE IS THE IMPORTANT THING

Maybe it's because John and I really do love each other very much and it comes over in the lessons (not purposely, but it does get pointed out to us!), that they feel they can ask us about it. Most kids are desperate to find that one person who is going to make them the happiest human being alive. Unfortunately, they look at their own parents' relationships and often see failure. Broken homes, two or three 'fathers' and being separated from your brother or sister doesn't help to convince you that it won't happen to you.

Do you know, Walt Disney films are still among the most popular in the world? And, like it or lump it, Barbara Cartland and Mills & Boon still outsell most seedy writers! Everyone is looking for love. Perhaps we would help more by discussing that issue with our kids? And then perhaps we won't have so many incidents like the one I remember so well from my schooldays, of my friend's mum coming home from shopping to find her husband and her daughter's boyfriend wandering aimlessly round the garden. When she asked what was wrong, they replied that Katy wasn't feeling well. On going up to her room, the mother found Katy in bed looking worried.

'What's wrong, love?' she asked.

Katy said, 'Mum, I'm going to have a baby.'

Her mother was aghast and couldn't think straight, she had no idea her daughter was pregnant. So she whispered, 'When?'

The shattering reply was . . . 'Now.'

Can you imagine the situation? And it happens all the time. Kids manage to conceal a pregnancy, and have even left the baby in a locker at school.

Let's start talking Love. Let's start talking For Ever and Ever

Amen. Let's start talking 'And they all lived happily ever after'. It can be done, if we start to teach kids the right way.

FRIENDS

Another important part of the relationships thing is friendship. Teenagers need a 'best friend', someone to confide in and to take confidence from. We all know people who have friends that have lasted a lifetime; whether they've moved away or stayed in the same street all their lives, that friendship is as close as ever.

MUTUAL APPRECIATION

I love the story of David and Jonathan for that very reason. Jonathan was an incredibly powerful best friend to have. He was willing to do just about anything for his friend David. The Bible says that he gave him his robe, his sword and his bow, and that's how it is with best friends. You want to give them trophies to show how much you appreciate them. I spoke to a girl the other day and said how much I liked her trousers, and she tossed her head and said, 'Oh they're not mine, they're my friend's.' Good friend, eh? An awful lot of values are learnt through having a good friend. Loyalty is something you can't buy, and sticking by a friend who's having a hard time is tough on both parties, but then, when he sticks by you in different circumstances, you begin to see the relevance of it all.

We often refer to God as a father figure and these days we are always being picked up on it because so many kids don't have fathers they can look up to . . . so maybe it's time to show them Jesus as the best friend they could ever have. The word 'relationship' has many different meanings. I've just looked some of them up in a thesaurus and come across words like: 'partnership', 'league', 'rapport' and 'joint venture'.

Great words, eh? All the kind of things you like to associate with best friends. So how much better if you could knit them together with Jesus and a brat?

SUMMARY

Add moral guidance to their knowledge.
Appreciate the pressure kids have to bear on this issue.
Stress the importance of love's qualities.
Encourage friendships in your group ... especially in the quieter ones; it will develop confidence.

Emotions

THERE are a few set answers to any question you ask a teenager. 'Don't know', 'S'all right', 'Nothing', and 'It's boring'. I know this can be frustrating at times, but if you can cast your mind back you will remember that you were exactly the same. *Moods and strops are highly delicate situations, which can become better or much much worse depending how you deal with them.*

THEY ARE TRYING TO GROW UP

In the chapter where we've let kids have their say, you will notice that one of the things that drive them crazy is when grown-ups say, 'Grow up!' Well, this is exactly what they are trying to do and they are well aware that they're not as grown-up as you! They are *growing* up! That's the whole point . . . they are not there yet . . . they are on their way!

Whatever your circumstances, if you are new at something, you are not going to get it right first time, or twentieth time, come to that. Imagine if you decided to go to art classes and brought home your very first sketch. Now, you know it's not very good – you've never done it before – but do you really need loads of people coming up to you saying, 'Oh, that's pretty wishy-washy, isn't it? Why didn't you use a stronger colour? I've got a friend who can draw much better than that! You want to do that again, that's what you want to do!'?

Now, honestly, how would that make you feel? You'd prob-ably get on the defensive straight away, you'd try to hide the sketch from anyone else and you'd probably tell that person to take a running jump. So the next person who comes along and says, 'What's that?' will find themselves faced with 'Nothing' as an answer. Already you've lost confidence in showing your 'creation' to anyone else. 'Well, what's it supposed to be?' they ask. 'I don't know,' you reply (thinking that if they can't see what it is, there's no point in trying to explain it).

It's quite possible that by now you will have lost interest in trying to draw ever again in your life. So the next time someone asks you, 'Why don't you go to art classes any more?' you will answer, 'It was boring.'

I hope that this is getting through in the way it's supposed to. Brats are still learning how to live, how to cope with turning into an adult – and it's hard, very hard to do. They are changing physically and emotionally at the same time and the last thing they need from you is to hear you tell your friends, 'It's a phase he's going through.'

The brat age is totally embarrassing. Your body gets out of control, it starts growing in all sorts of weird places . . . and not all at the same time! The opposite sex becomes something that is of interest to you all of a sudden, and you have no idea how to cope with it. Your emotional state is pulling you five different ways at once . . . and somewhere in the middle of that are adults telling you to 'grow up'.

TRY NOT TO ADD TO THEIR INSECURITIES.

This kind of change in the life of a brat will make them feel very insecure. What they need right now is an awful lot of understanding, patience and encouragement. Sounds easy enough, doesn't it? But unfortunately, most adults' idea of encouragement and the brat's idea of encouragement, are miles apart. Most kids of this age will not respond well to hugs from their parents. They see this as embarrassing, and yet they will respond sometimes to hugs from a friend or leader. Check out which works in your case and stick by it! It might be hard, when you've been used to physical contact with a young teen, to see them move away from you . . . but if you want them back . . . let them move!

It's easy to put down but not so easy to build up.

Laughing is another embarrassing thing. Mocking clothes and haircuts is not a good idea. When you feel insecure in the first place, you can well do without people pointing at you. Now and again it's a good idea to dig out your own photos of yourself as a teenager and show them to your youth group. Let's all have a good laugh at the state of *you!* Discussing clothes and haircuts in *your* day is a wonderful way of saying, 'Look, I went through this too!' You'll probably find they'll end up asking if you've kept any of those hideous fashions, so that they can try them on!

Along with all the spots, breaking voices and the race to get the first bra, will come an attitude to their faith.

QUESTIONS AND DOUBTS ARE HEALTHY.

They will want to question everything and that's great. They have come to the stage where what their parents say to them isn't good enough, and what you tell them isn't good enough either. When kids are very young, they start pointing at things and saying, 'What's that?' and whatever answer you give them will be followed by the response 'Why?' This is a never-ending routine and I've seen it drive people round the bend, but it's a natural response for a growing child. *Now*, when that child becomes a brat, the questions get much more awkward. Nothing is going to be good enough, just because you say it is. Remember, you also told them about the tooth fairy and Father Christmas! (By the way, that's fine . . .) But now, they are at the age where they have to sort out fiction from fantasy, and they are going to do it for themselves!

What an adult thinks is going to be irrelevant by and large and you just have to sweat it out and pray that, when the time is right, they will actually turn to you.

This is the stage when they start to make outrageous statements and you have to cope with that.

'I'm never going to work in an office. I'm going to be a tour operator in Barbados.'

'I'll never cut my hair and I'm always going to wear these jeans.'

'You don't know the first thing about life! I'm not going to waste time like you've done. I'm going to see the world and find a cure for cancer.'

'I'll leave home as soon as I can, and get a flat with a decent CD player.'

'I don't need money. I'm going to live from day to day and just get work when I need it. I've seen other people do it.'

There is really no point in getting in a fix over these comments, as they are going to change once a fortnight anyway. And we all know that the best way to drive people towards something you don't want them to do, is to say, 'Oh no you're not, young lady!'

When a child is very young you try hard to protect him from doing stupid things like putting his tiny hands near the fire. 'Ohh! Hot! Hot! Nasty! Burn!' you cry and take the hand away before he feels the effects. The child's mind is still thinking 'Why? Why can't I do that? What's going to happen when I do?' And, because of these feelings, there comes a day when he can't contain himself any more and, while you are out of the room, he ventures near the fireguard and finds out for himself the meaning of the word 'Hot'.

Of course we have to protect young people from making mistakes that can wreck their lives, but *it's good to understand how they feel*, so we know how to approach them.

ALWAYS BE PREPARED TO LISTEN.

Whenever a brat approaches you with a screwball idea – *listen to him*. Don't write it off. The chances are he's not thought through how to pay for this mega-flat he's going to own the minute he leaves school . . . but rather than downing his ideas, listen to them. Recall the things that *you* were going to do when you got your freedom. Take the chance that this person is giving you to share in his dreams . . . if you laugh in his face, he may never bother to tell you anything again.

'PAT ANSWERS' ARE NOT THE ANSWER!

Along with the dreams and ambitions come the questions. The questions that demand proper answers.

When we are taking lessons in schools, we often get asked to do these kind of forum things, where the kids fire questions at us and we're expected to come up with all the answers. Over the years, we found it was much more beneficial to actually take time to answer the questions properly, or even say, 'I don't know', than give them some bland clever retort.

Kids are not into smart answers.

When they ask, 'How do you know there's a God?' A smart answer about not being able to see electricity but it's still there and if you put your hand in an electric socket you'll find that God's real too . . .is OK and may get a few laughs, but at the end of the day, you've not left that kid with a very satisfying answer to what could have been a serious question. So these days we try to be more open and honest with our answers and find that they respond in a much more grown-up manner. They appreciate truth. 'I don't know' is as much a valid answer as anything else. *When we try to be clever, they find it patronizing and belittling to them –* and they're right!

As I said earlier, while the hormones are going on the rampage inside their bodies their faith is being questioned too. Up till now, they may have gone along with what their parents have taught them, or what they've heard in church or Sunday school. But now, they are old enough to think for themselves, to reason and question, and a whole new ball game comes to the front. And the bottom line is this – *You can't believe in Jesus just because someone else told you it's true!*

KIDS NEED TO MAKE UP THEIR OWN MINDS.

Being a Christian is a personal thing, and no matter how good you are, and how Christian your parents and friends are, it won't make the slightest difference to your own life. We go through this with Christian kids week in, week out. There comes a point when you have to make a decision for yourself.

This is especially difficult for kids who have parents who are leaders in a church, or evangelists or speakers. These kids have been brought up with the Gospel, they know it inside out and backwards. They have heard every inspiring preacher in the world and been to so many conferences it'd make your head spin! Now, their problem is twofold: not only does everyone expect them to follow in their parents' footsteps, but they expect them to be mega-Christians too! These kids have an impossible reputation to live up to! And they all come to the Brat Pack stage where they have to make their own decisions. What your parents are, or what your friends are, is irrelevant. Some of them go through the most awful stage of trying to keep up this reputation – even though they have never made a proper decision for Jesus, ever!

Now, these kids and your everyday church kids have one thing in common. They need to work it out for themselves. That's why they ask such awkward questions. That's why they get stroppy and moody. These things have to be worked out! They need *time*, they need *space*, so don't crowd them too much. Just make sure you're around when they want to make that decision for themselves.

Loads of church kids have said to us, 'I have put my hand up at meetings. I've been out to talk to someone . . . but it doesn't seem real. I can't make it real!' True, you can't *make* it real! When Jesus comes into a person's life, He comes into *their* life . . . not their parents', family's or friends', just theirs, and I think this is where a lot of kids come unstuck. They don't make Jesus Lord of their lives, they are just doing what's expected of them. You know, the family like going for long walks, so you go with them – you don't particularly like long walks, but it's something they do, so you go along with it. Well, you can't treat Jesus like that. He's either Lord of All, or not Lord at all!

If you get an opportunity to talk to the kids under your wing . . . then please explain this to them. It's only when they make Jesus their own personal Lord that it will become real. This decision has to be theirs and theirs alone and cannot be influenced by anyone else. Jesus died for each brat personally, and that's the only way it works.

It's normally at this age that a teenager comes to grips with all these things. His character. His body. His emotions. His future. And most importantly, His Lord.

Come to terms with when to stand back and when to be there. It's difficult, I know, because you only want to help . . . but try hard never to be a hindrance to what God is doing in their lives. Give them space.

SUMMARY

Don't say things that belittle the kids.
Build kids up. They need the encouragement.
Listen to their crazy ideas.
Give them more than a pat answer.
Make sure you are around when it's their 'decision' time.

CHAPTER THIRTEEN

'I Don't Like
Sundays'

I T'S amazing how interesting feet can be! Or a bit of fluff
caught on your jacket, or *anything* that can keep your eyes
away from the minister in front of you or the disapproving
looks of the people around you. Yes, we're in church!

We've gone back to the nineteenth century, it's traditions
and backgrounds. It's one of life's great mysteries, is the
Church. It's almost superstitious the way the Church won't
move forward into the 1900s let alone the 1990s! What's going
to happen if we let the Church use modern equipment, music,
and words? Maybe it's going to be even worse than stepping
on a crack in the pavement, or walking under a ladder!

Well, really . . . it does drive you crazy at times. To John and
me it is perfectly obvious that kids are having a tremendously
hard time coping with churchgoing and we as church members
are going little or nothing about it.

THE TRIALS OF CHURCH FOR A
TEENAGER

Next Sunday, when you go to your service, have a look around
you and put yourself in the position of your young people.
Don't kid yourself, look properly with an open mind. I'll tell
you what you will see. You'll see kids who don't mind coming
up to the front and reading the Bible, kids who will even get up
and do some kind of drama . . . but you won't find many kids

singing! When 'worship time' comes around, it's time to find the jacket fluff. Yes, I know you enjoy it, but your kids don't! No, they don't! It's a fact, kids don't sing any more. They don't sing in assembly, they don't sing in music lessons ... they don't sing!

As we are compiling this book, we can tell you that kids will chant at football matches, rap to a decent beat, and wail the odd anthem dedicated to someone or something they like ... but they very rarely sing. We are actually back to the times when brats would rather yell 'And also with you!' as a response, than they would sing a chorus. By the time this book reaches the printers, anything could have happened! But what we seem to *fail to recognize is that we must stay relevant*!

Worship, I know, is only a small part of the problem, but if we can get to grips with it as a *problem* then maybe we can direct the answer to other parts of the Church and its service. You see, I know that you like the worship in your church – and because of this you can't understand how it could possibly be that anyone else doesn't. Can I take five minutes of your time to try and explain something to you? Thanks.

Anyone under the age of fifty has now been brought up hearing some kind of music with a beat. Most have been brought up with rock music on the radio. So, as far as we are concerned, as long as it's got a beat – it's modern! Which of course is rubbish. But it has created this mentality among parents and youth leaders, that the kids are going to love the worship because someone plays the drums! As we write this, the current music trend is for 'house' and 'rave'. (Bear with me ...) Now, most rock music has its accent on the second and fourth beat of the bar, thus creating the 'rock' feel. However, today's music has its accent on all four beats of the bar and creates an entirely new 'feel' for dancing. What I'm basically saying is ... if you try to dance in today's style with yesterday's music ... you fall over! And really, this is a very small problem compared to others ... but believe me, it's awkward for kids.

And it's the same for such a lot of our traditional

Christianity. If you try to make sense of a traditional Bible – you fall over! If you try to listen to a sermon that's more than twenty minutes long – you keel over!

All right, I'll stop the list of complaints and get on with the problem.

LOOKING FOR REALITY

Brats are only interested in things that are real and will change their lives. A lot of our Christianity is tradition. A while ago we were in Holland and the first time we went there, we had all sorts of problems with the fact that Christians smoke. I don't mean that they just smoke now and again, I mean an awful lot of them roll their own in the prayer meeting! And they seem to drink an awful lot more . . . we played in quite a few churches that keep a well stocked bar! We found that quite difficult to handle, especially when we were inviting young schoolkids along to their buildings. On the other hand, when they say grace, it's a whole new ball game from the way we see it. For a start they say it at the end of the meal and then they have a Bible reading followed by a short discussion on what the reading meant and then there's a prayer about it.

I mentioned this to one particular Christian girl, and told her how hard I found it to watch people smoke and pray and she just smiled and said, 'Ah yes, but Sue, we find it just as hard that you come into our church wearing make-up!'

Wow! And there were we thinking that *they* were the 'offensive' ones, when all the time my make-up was winding them up too! Gradually, we began to realize that an awful lot of what we call *'Christian'* is in fact *'tradition'* or *'culture'* and actually nothing to do with believing in Jesus at all!

Which brings us neatly back to our own church services. How much of what happens in your church is 'Christian' and how much is 'culture'?

There's an easy way to find out. If it doesn't change your life

... it's culture. And this is what the kids find so frustrating. So much of church is just about tradition and there's not enough about Jesus. And the bottom line is that young people today have a *great interest in real things*, and in schools we are always being asked questions about our lives.

'Why don't you try and have a hit record instead of just singing songs about God?'

'What has God ever done for you?'

'Could anything make you give up your faith?'

THE IMPORTANT ISSUES

These are not questions about a building, about standing up and sitting down, or about how many times we go to church. These are genuine questions about how our lives are affected by the faith we have in God. Kids at school are not interested in whether we sit in pews or on the floor, whether we renew stained glass windows or drink communion wine from a gold or plastic cup. They *just want to know if Christianity is worth the effort*, and because of this they watch every move John and I make. If they don't see something life-changing in what we do, then they will write Christianity off along with politics, the weather, school and anything else they can't rely on. *Is that what we want?* And the other thing is that as these teenagers become adults ... we are gonna find ourselves with a church full of dissatisfied middle-aged people ... and I think you'll find that *that* is happening already!

It's true to say that in the 'old days' the Church had a very successful time. John and I were at a church a few years ago where they have only just taken down the crutches and walking sticks from the walls. Unfortunately, these discarded walking aids were mementoes from a revival that happened in the 1930s!! We can't possibly expect today's kids to live from stories of healings and conversions that happened before they were born. *They need to see it for themselves!*

We aren't even holding our own.

We are in a situation these days, where we can't keep the kids who have grown up in the Church, let alone bring in any new ones! The facts and figures tell us that 300 kids of Brat Pack age are leaving our churches every week ... *what are we going to do about it?*

Recently in New Zealand, Christian kids were consulted about the kind of meeting they would like to see happen.

Bear in mind that this was more a kind of youth meeting after church, not a church service. Most of the kids came to the same conclusion – they didn't want loads of singing. They didn't mind having Christian bands and solo artists, but worship songs were awkward because they wanted to bring in their non-Christian friends and they knew that the choruses *wouldn't be relevant to people who couldn't praise a God they didn't believe in.* They were quite happy to have a preacher, as long as he could preach in three or four different stages throughout the evening, rather than all at once. Maybe a decent drama that caught up on the evening's theme and plenty of videos that could also be stopped and started in much the same way as the preacher.

The youth leaders decided to go along with their ideas, and now over 500 kids meet together after church for this youth-style service. *Hang on!* We are not giving you licence to carry on with your dull service and do a 'youth service' as an alternative! No way! Young teens need to be in with other people so that they can grow. We all need to be with each other, so don't use the youth service a a cop-out.

I'm just telling you what I know has worked.

Common Ground

It's vital that *we learn from each other* and I know that in our old church in Guernsey, the older people very much appreciated what the young people had to offer, and vice versa. It had to be worked on, but once it was we found that old and young had things in common. We started to have our youth meetings at the houses of the older ladies in our church. They were delighted to bake us cakes and fill us full of tea, and they loved to hear the voices of excited teenagers in their front rooms once again. It reminded them of their own sons and daughters (now all grown and left home . . .) and filled their homes with sounds that hadn't been there for many years.

This type of social event paved the way for others, and we gradually started to learn about the people in our church. There was the old man who had collected coins all his life, suddenly he found a young kid of eighteen who was just starting up a collection himself . . . they became firm friends. And then the two elderly spinsters who used to scream themselves silly playing a stupid board game with four of our young people. And the first time you see an old age pensioner on a computer game . . . well, you know you're getting there.

I suppose it's called 'breaking down barriers', but it's all about getting the church together so that this ridiculous stumbling block of tradition can be removed. It has to go, I'm afraid, there's no alternative. We have to remove the barrier before The Brat Pack remove themselves instead.

SUMMARY

Stay relevant.
Get reality.
Our culture affects our faith.
Show kids Christianity is worth the effort – in spite of its communication problems.
Teenagers need adult guidance and company.
The Church needs their energy and freshness.
Influence your church on their behalf.

CHAPTER FOURTEEN

Ideas for Action

ICE-BREAKERS, games, quizzes . . . call these what you will, you can never have enough of them. Some work all the time, others just work at the time! We found that when we wanted to think of new ideas and refashion old ones, the main problem was *finding things where everyone could join in*.

Games for all

Now, I know you don't need that all the time, but we tend to find that kids get bored if they have to watch a team of six having all the fun and they just get to sit there. For this reason 'teams' were invented – at least you get to cheer them!

Another reason we went overboard to sort out games that everyone can join in, is because we are constantly working with kids in their hundreds, as well as groups of thirty or fifty.

The first game we ever tried in an effort to get everyone joining in, was called the *Row Game* – and it was a riot!

The basic idea was to split the audience down the middle by making an aisle, and picking someone from the front row and asking them to choose a question worth one, two, or three points. They had to answer it by themselves and if they got it right, the whole side moved up one, two, or three rows. This caused total chaos, trying to shift maybe 200 kids per side. The easiest way (as the kids found out) was to climb over the chairs into the row in front! As it happened, the first time we did this game we had a young boy in a wheelchair who had the time of his life being pushed around the hall at an enormous pace by his very enthusiastic new-found friends!

The winning team are the ones who get back to their original seats in the front first. To avoid cheating, we made a few people in the original front rows wear huge silly sunglasses, so that we could see where they were.

We have found that 'teams' are very important to get the excitement going – but the names that the teams are given are even more important. They must sound good and roll off the tongue well so that they can shout for their teams. A few years ago we used the names of cars for a particular event. Chevys, Rollers and Mercedes. Now, Chevys and Rollers are great names to chant, but Mercedes, much as it is a great car, was a lousy name to yell. The result of this kind of faux pas is that no one wants to be in the Mercedes team and everyone keeps changing sides.

Last week we were at a youth weekend and were given the theme of prisons. The talks were based around being bound by your guilt, freedom, breaking your chains . . . that sort of thing. So John and I sat around for ages working on names for two teams. All the really good ones were a bit dodgy – like Muggers and Ramraiders(!) – and all the others only seemed to have one exciting name and one boring one, like Strangeways (which is good to chant) and Boreham Wood (which isn't!) In the end we used the thesaurus on my computer and asked it for alternative names for Prison. Wonderful! . . . It came up with Coolers and Slammers!

Both words had great connotations and as the weekend was mainly with boys, it worked extremely well.

THEMES ADD SPARKLE

If you don't have a theme for the event you are running, you can always get the kids to come up with their own names . . . but you are liable to end up with teams called 'The Sewer Rats' and 'Slime Dragons' . . . but there you are.

A theme is always a good idea as you can *base the whole programme around it*, making sure that the games fit in with the theme. This usually means that the kids rapidly latch on to it and are ahead of you pretty quickly. Even with a theme as ordinary as 'colours', we've found that within a day the kids are arriving dressed in their colour and carrying no end of mascots – huge green fluffy frogs, red trolls and yellow inflatable bananas! Of course, the motive behind this is that anything remotely worthy wins points for their team. Young teens are naturally competitive and like to identify, so this gives them a chance to do both.

I mentioned 'chants' earlier on. This is another good idea to get the kids supporting their gang. Chants vary a great deal and usually start with an older team leader composing something really easy like 'We're the Rollers, we're the best, we are gonna beat the rest!' The whole team clap and chant this as loudly as possible, so as to smother the sound of any other team doing the same thing. The chants then get more and more ambitious as time goes on . . . we've had banners the length of the hall, words sung to a popular chart song, conga lines and incredibly intricate dance routines! And just think . . . this is all before you've started on the games!

GAMES, ACTIVITIES

OK, we have split the games up into three categories. Ones that can be played by everybody, ones that get played by teams, and finally, the messy ones! Some of these games you might know well, and some of them we have made up as we've seen the need. They are not particularly outstanding – they just work! We have spent hours sorting out great ideas and making extraordinary props and backdrops, only to watch the idea flop the first time it's tried, and then dished up a really easy idea and watched it fly! (If at first you don't succeed! . . .)

GAMES FOR ALL

ABC Game (An exercise in peer pressure.)

There are various ways of doing this. Three parts of the room are denoted as A, B and C; usually by way of posters or something. Now, the next bit we have usually worked out from a Bible dictionary. Just find a really awkward name and give it two false meanings and its true one. E.g. BOTCH . . . Is it A, a stew or casserole of lamb; is it B, a mixture of boiling oil and grease; or is it C, a nasty boil or blemish on the skin? The answer is actually C and few get it right because, in a way, it sounds a bit obvious . . . like you've made it up. Whereas a casserole sounds more feasible as does the oil and grease.

When you've read out your three definitions, you give your kids one minute to run to the part of the room they think holds the correct answer. Those who get it wrong sit down and those who were right get another go. You can play this out until you have maybe three or four left . . . or even an outright winner. You can add more excitement to the game by winding the kids up into thinking they've won . . . e.g. 'Well, a lot of people went to B, hardly any to C and just a few to A. By the way, A – you're wrong! And C, did you really think it could possibly be a boil?? Just as well really, because You are Right!!'

ABC Secrets (Getting to know your leader better.)

This is the same format, but can be played one of two ways. Have a chat with your leaders/helpers and find out if they have any hidden secrets that the kids wouldn't know about. By this, we mean things they did as kids, or something you wouldn't expect them to have done. For example, we played this game with some leaders at Spring Harvest and found that in our midst we had . . . Someone who had trained the black horse for the bank TV commercial . . . someone who had been arrested by the police for armed robbery and someone else who had sat in a shop window in a bath completely naked! OK! Own-up time . . . the guy who was arrested by the police actually was a case of mistaken identity – but pretty frightened to be slammed up against his car with guns at his throat! And the girl who sat in the bath was only three at the time, and her dad had taken her into the shop to look around the bathroom department!

Happily, your kids don't know any of this and will have a lot of fun finding out who is telling the truth. The game is played by three leaders/helpers coming forward and reading from a card like this: 'Hello, my name is Ben and I was once arrested for armed robbery.' And the next person: 'Hello, my name is Sarah and I was once arrested for armed robbery.' Once your three suspects have announced themselves, the two teams (or whatever) are allowed to put their hands up and ask clever questions to try and outwit the contestants. This is made all the more difficult by the fact that the leader who is telling the truth *must stick to it*, but the other two can lie through their teeth!

After three or four questions a side, the teams have to take a vote by a show of hands. The leader telling the truth then has to step forward. This game is a lot of fun, and you certainly learn things about people!!

The other way of playing the game is to get the kids to run to A, B or C to decide who's telling the truth.

Bingo! (Getting to know each other better.)
Oooh err! Don't panic, it's just a name! This game is a nice way of helping your kids to get to know each other. A lot of the time, they tend to only really know the few friends they are always with and this gets them talking to everyone. You need

a sheet of paper with squares drawn on it. Say, twelve squares, four along and three down. Black out three of them at random and then number the others one to nine. Now, you need to write things by the numbers like: 1. Has grade one piano. 2. Has a Take That single. etc., etc. The paper then needs to be photostated for however many people you think will be there, and given out to each kid. The idea is that they must collect a signature in each vacant box. They can use their own signature once, but the others must be signed by eight individuals. You must go up to people and ask them a question, e.g. 'Have you got grade one piano? . . . you can't just go up and say, 'Can you sign any of these?' The winner is the first person to get his paper full, with nine signatures. N.B. This game works very well with a large number, as the confusion and noise help people to approach each other.

Ankle Balloons (Fun game.)

Virtually self explanatory! This needs to be prepared beforehand and then put in another room if possible. You need two balloons per person. (Again, the more people the merrier, but you might need to buy a balloon pump if there's over fifty!!) Blow the balloons up and attach a piece of wool (not nylon) or string to each balloon. The string needs to be about two feet long. Give each kid two balloons and tell them to tie one round each ankle so that the balloons can blow about freely. It is important not to let your balloons burst at this stage.

When everyone is sufficiently tied to their balloons you can get a countdown going. When you hit 'zero' everyone has to try and stamp on everyone else's balloons, whilst keeping their own intact! It's good fun to play and great fun to watch. Some people go all out to burst as many balloons as possible and some just try and keep out of the way of having their own balloons burst. The winner(s) are the last remaining inflated balloon owners.

Silver Treasure Hunt (How to give away money . . .)

Treasure hunts are always popular, but definitely more so this way. For this game you need a pile of loose change.

Get your helpers to off-load all their change on you; the more change, the better the game. In amongst the change you need two one pound coins, four fifty pences, loads of ten and five ps and millions of ones and twos. The bugbear of the game is that they all have to be individually wrapped in tinfoil. This can take quite a time, so it needs to be done the day before.

On the day of the event, you go around the hall/room, placing the silver in places where it can just about be seen. Windowsills, radiators, behind pipes, cracks in the wall, etc. As yet we haven't had anyone come into the hall and pick up a piece of silver paper wondering what it was . . . so it's fairly safe to have it all arranged before the programme starts. But it does have to be the first game.

We have used this hunt at youth meetings and also at week-ends . . . and there's something about the fact that *there's money inside the silver paper* that makes the kids *really go for it*! We normally say something like 'Around the room there are things hidden. Stay where you are until we say go . . . BUT! Wrapped in silver paper is money. There are loads of one and two ps . . . but there are also some fives and tens and even four fifty pences and two one pound coins! Now, whatever you find . . . you keep . . . GO!'

Do you know, we had kids searching for a whole weekend because one fifty pence piece was unaccounted for!! And they did actually find it! We were in the Lake District and were using the garden surrounding the centre as the place to hunt. The fifty pence piece was in the pond, by the way!

Body Bridges (Contact game.)

A bit more physical this one. Split into groups of twelve, and try to build a bridge across the floor using only certain parts of the body. For instance: the only parts that can touch the floor are five feet, two backsides, six hands, two elbows and four knees, Kids enjoy getting into this tangled mess – if only to prove they can do it!

You can also try giving them a word pertaining to the theme and get them to spell the word with their bodies. It's interesting to see how they see it in their minds.

These are just a few ideas, but at least we know that they work well. We always try very hard to use *games where no one feels embarrassed to join in*. Our aim isn't to make them feel afraid but to get them relaxed and enjoying the programme.

VOLUNTARY GAMES (SPECTATOR GAMES)

When it comes to games played by volunteers, the rules do change slightly, basically because *if you are the type to volunteer* then you're usually also the type *not to care what people think*! For some reason, lots of these games have been partially nicked from TV programmes and, at the time of going to print, these were the kind of things going on:

Whose Line? (A bit of a drama.)
You need to write out loads of four-line dialogues for this. Very ordinary things like:
1. What's for tea?
2. Sausages, chips and beans.
1. Have you got any vinegar?
2. No, but there's plenty of tomato sauce.

As you can see, these dialogues are for two people. So you ask for two volunteers who think they can act. Now, everyone thinks they are good at this, so we don't normally find ourselves short.

Put all the different pieces of paper with the dialogues on, into a bag or envelope and then ask them to pick one out. On doing this, you must then give them a couple of minutes to read through the script, decide who is going to be number one and who's going to be number two. Then ask them to play out the sketch as normally as they can. Even this usually receives a cheer from the audience, who love to see their friends doing something on stage. Once they have acted their parts, you then present them with another envelope, this one contains different types of styles, e.g. Cowboys, *Thunderbirds*, Opera, Guns 'n' Roses, very slow, etc.

They now have to re-enact the dialogue using the style they have picked out of the envelope. This causes much mirth amongst the kids and can sometimes be the turning point in a young teenager's acting career!

Blind Date Types. (Using technology.)

The candid-type games once again are fairly embarrassing, but if you volunteer, you volunteer! We have seen the actual *Blind Date* game work very well, but only with the use of a bit of technology . . . (for more info see the chapter on Hi-Tech!) These days there's always someone in your group who has access to a camcorder, and to do Blind Date properly it's a good idea to have one, plus facilities to project onto a screen so that your audience can see what's going on. First of all, you take your three boys into a different room so that they can't hear what's going on, and then you interview the girl candidate. After this, you put the girl in a different room (or the wings of the curtain) and bring out the boys. The camcorder is then set up pointing at the girl's face; she is also given a microphone. So now, while you are interviewing the boys, you can see the reaction of the girl as well as hearing her questions. If you have someone technically minded, you can get them to alter the pitch of the girl's voice so that she is unrecognized. Needless to say you need a fairly large audience, otherwise you would spot who was missing.

The other way to play this type of game is in the form of the old *Mr & Mrs*, but instead of giving it romantic inclinations, you can change the atmosphere by getting two best friends to volunteer.

How Well Do I Know My Best Friend?

We usually play the record 'Better than I know myself' by Cliff Richard, to introduce this game. Because you are interviewing best friends, you can keep the questions fairly low-key, e.g. 'Does she prefer a beefburger to a Chinese?' 'Does she like to stay in and watch TV or to go out?' 'Would she lend you a fiver if you were broke?' Yes, many a happy friendship has ended this way!!

Seriously, though, just in case you don't know the gist of the game . . . one person goes out of the room and the other person is questioned about the one outside. Then the one outside is brought back in, and the same questions are asked again . . . it's amazing how many times the answers differ, and how stupid you feel when you've confidently said that your friend would lend you a fiver, and then when they ask her she says 'No chance!'

Karaoke (For the poseurs in your group.)

Yes, I'm afraid it's still popular. Karaoke is the art of singing along to a backing track whilst reading the words to the song. It's a hideous form of entertainment which gives hours of fun to everyone!

We tend to have a Karaoke night, rather than just a five-minute set in a programme, but either way can work well. We type out a list of every song that we have on tape, and put a copy of this on every table. Then when the kids come in, we serve coffee and they sit around daring each other to have a go. This generally lapses into 'I will if you will' and you end up with around three or four all getting up together to sing. Songs like 'Rocking All Over the World' and 'Wild Thing' are always big favourites, and before you know it everyone is a megastar!

The main event of the night is when some kid eventually strikes on the idea of the leaders singing 'Rock Around the Clock' or even worse 'My Way'. So be warned, OK? The real star of the show is you!

Marshmallows

I wonder who invented marshmallows, and whether they realized at the time that they would be the most popular form of sweets to play games with?

The most popular game of all time has to be 'Chubby Bunnies'. I still have no idea why it's such a winner, but it's the kind of game that people will volunteer for all night long! And as we turn to this game I suppose we should have the next heading . . .

Messy Games (You and they will love it.)

'Chubby Bunnies' consists of finding four volunteers to come and stand at the front of the hall. You will need plenty of packets of marshmallows, some plastic carrier bags, some kitchen roll, and if possible, a microphone.

The idea is that you give all your contestants two marshmallows which they must place in their mouths and not chew. Then, you point a mike at them and ask them to say 'Chubby Bunnies'. At first, it's fairly easy to say, but as you increase the dosage of marshmallows, it gets more and more disgusting. Fellas and girls alike have an inbuilt desire to keep going with ten, twelve, fourteen marshmallows in their mouths. It looks as disgusting as you think it does . . . and by now the plastic bags come into play. When a contestant starts waving their arms about and looking distressed, it's generally taken to mean that they would like to dispose of the contents of their mouth very quickly and for that you need someone to rush up with an open carrier bag! It really is important to keep an eye on the proceedings and to stop anyone who you think has had enough – even if they want to carry on. Adults, of course, usually last a little longer, but eight–twelve is a very good score. (Although we have seen someone manage sixteen . . . but we'd rather forget it!)

Chocolate Marshmallows

And still on the subject of marshmallows . . . there are hundreds of permutations of this next game. Four people lie on the floor with four people standing at their shoulders. The four people on the floor need to be wearing plastic bin liners. The people standing are holding a dish of marshmallows which are then ceremoniously covered in as much chocolate sauce as you can get in the dish. The idea is for the kids standing up to drop the marshmallows into the mouths of the kids on the floor. It's a nice idea to do a countdown and then stop just before you get to 'one', hit your head and say you've forgotten the blindfolds! So now the game consists of some blindfolded people aiming at mouths they can't see, with the help of a yelling audience and a rather worried kid on the receiving end . . . Still, at least it tastes nice! Unlike this next game . . .

Choke the Yolk (The worst of all.)

The fun of the game is wandering around hardware shops trying to find a piece of flexible see-through tubing. It does exist, some plumbing departments have it. Anyway, when you have your tubing, you bring on two willing contestants who hold either end of the tube. They bend it so it forms a curve at the bottom, and then an egg is cracked into it. The egg floats around in the 'U' of the tubing, looking revolting. The kids then have to take two deep breaths and blow down the tube. Yes, awful thought, isn't it! It's not so bad if you are both blowing down the tube at the same time – the egg tends to stray up one side a bit and then up the other. The disaster happens when one kid really belts at it, and the kid at the other end is just starting to take a breath!

Catchers (For the baseball freaks.)

This is much more sensible . . . well, sort of. It needs to be played outdoors. Pretend to the kids that you are going to see how far people can catch and throw a ball. This in itself brings out the egotists. Two kids have to stand facing each other, just a little apart, and then one throws the ball to the other; if he catches it he takes a step back. The same thing then happens to the other guy. You can keep taking steps back every time the ball is caught and gradually get right across a field before the ball is caught.

Once they have the idea . . . bring on the box of eggs! *The game now takes on a dramatic change*. There are definite ways to catch an egg – if you push out your hands towards it you will smash it quite easily; if you hold your hands in front of your body and go with the flow it will smash into you! So what you have to do is to catch the egg, going with the flow, to the side of you. But, of course, it's much more fun if you don't tell the kids this.

We did on one occasion play this game inside a marquee and two kids managed to keep the game going so well that we had to open the flaps of the tent. You can imagine what it looked like . . . all the audience could see was this egg whizzing in and out of the tent! Eventually they threw it too high and it fried on the spotlights. (Not such a good idea, but amusing to smell fried eggs for the rest of the programme!)

Catapults (For the storm-troopers in your group.)

Another good outside game, although different versions can be played indoors. This one takes a bit more time as you have to make the catapults . . . but once you've got them, you can use them for ever. Now, here I should mention that we are not talking ordinary little catapults like the ones Dennis the Menace uses. We are talking catapults that take three people to fire! (Hey, come on, you want the kids to have fun, don't you!!?)

The catapult consists of two sturdy pieces of wood with the kind of elastic you use on a roof rack attached to them. They meet in the middle by way of something bowl-shaped (we used some plastic colanders). To actually fire these things, you need two people holding on to the upright pieces of wood, and one person to hold on to the colander and walk backwards until the catapult is stretched to its limit. Worried yet?

At the other end of the field you need lots of kids holding a large sheet for catching water balloons in. Oh, sorry, didn't I mention the water balloons?

The tamer version of this is to play it indoors with bean bags and fishing nets. The principle is the same. You have two teams competing to see who can collect the most water balloons or beanbags in a given length of time.

Wine Making (Non-alcoholic of course!)

We'll finish with this one. Again, I have no idea why people in their right minds volunteer for things like this, especially when they have seen it done and know what they are in for!

For this game you will need two pounds of grapes and two contestants. They are each given a bowl and a bunch of grapes. They then have to take their shoes and socks off and tread the grapes, with the aim of seeing who can make the most 'wine'. Amidst a thousand jokes on smelly feet and funny-looking things floating in the wine, the contest continues. When the kids think they can tread no more, the contents of the bowls are poured into wine glasses. At this point I should tell you that it looks disgusting. Usually it's a kind of pale grey slush with pips and bits of sock fluff in. The wine is now measured to find the winner, who is congratulated wholeheartedly on his 'feat'. Then you ask the audience what they think should happen to the loser. Strangely enough, drinking the wine seems a very popular suggestion at this stage! If you are feeling really mean, then the loser has to drink the winner's wine!! (N.B. Just a sip! Don't make them drink it all . . . unless they are real poseurs!)

Now honestly, can you imagine anyone actually volunteering to be part of that . . . having seen what happens?

So there you have it, just a few ideas to get your young people involved. It would be great if you could take these ideas and work on new angles. Someone once said to us that *if you think up the wildest idea you can, and the most outrageous game in your head . . . then you will just be hitting the tip of the kind of thing that kids like.* And it's true. I know a guy who played a game called The Lion Hunt with his kids. They used a forest, and the idea was to follow the clues through the 'jungle' until you finally got to the middle where the 'lion' was . . . except that he had actually hired a real live lion and its keeper. I mean, can you imagine these kids' faces when they leapt through the undergrowth to be faced with the real McCoy chained to a tree!!?

So don't worry that your game might be a bit over the top for the kids . . . chances are that will never ever happen!

SUMMARY

Teams and themes add sparkle.
Young teens are naturally competitive.
Choose games that help kids mix.
But – don't embarrass the shy ones.
Let your imagination run wild.

Weekends Away

W HAT can be said about youth weekends? If you've never tried taking your kids away for a few days, let me try and explain what you are in for when you do!

OUT IN THE COUNTRY

There are many types of places where young people are very welcome in numbers of twenty to a hundred. Most of them are old mansions in the country, the kind of place that lends itself to having masses of kids swinging from trees and screaming and yelling over acres of countryside. Some of these centres will provide beds, sheets, and blankets plus food and people to instruct you on abseiling. Others will just be very basic . . . bring your own sleeping bag and form two dormitories in two largish halls, bring your own goodies and try to cook them on a stove made for three people!

Now, at this stage, I must warn you that the only people who are not going to like the 'sleeping on the floor' routine are the youth leaders! It doesn't seem to make much difference to the kids – mainly because of the other thing that makes a weekend away what it is – and *that's* that *nobody sleeps*! Yes, for the whole weekend, you are going to count yourself incredibly fortunate if you manage to shut your eyes for more than three hours a night!

Well, come on, can you imagine fifty excited kids wanting to do anything as boring as sleep, when they're away from their parents, home and all known authority? (Except you, and you're their friend anyway . . .!) Anyway, I was trying to tell you what a youth weekend consists of:

They are mainly broken up into three parts: the *physical*, the *mental* and the *spiritual*. Every centre is good for a particular sport or activity. Some have great facilities for water sports like canoeing and swimming, etc. Others, as I said earlier, have experts to take your gang on hikes, mountain-climbing expeditions and potholing. Yet again, you may find that some places are set in a farm where the kids can pick fruit or watch lambs being born and learn how to milk cows! There's always something that makes the activities really special, and you need to decide what kind of group you are taking away, *before* you choose the action!

It's a relaxed time to open up.

They will also need some *time to themselves*, this is where the 'mental' stuff comes in. You need to be around during those times. It's the time when they wander around the fields or whatever thinking about life, the universe and everything, and it's a great opportunity to talk to them on a one-to-one basis. Once kids are outside their own natural environment, they open up. The defences come down pretty quickly and they tell you things they wouldn't dream of telling you at home.

The spiritual part is usually where John and I come in. Making a session work when all around you is very attractive, is a challenge in itself. Most leaders want between three and five sessions over a long weekend. Generally there's one on the night everyone arrives, a kind of 'getting to know you' session, then one the next morning and one the same evening. The final day is usually a mish-mash of session and concerts . . . some by us and some by them! It's almost traditional to have a concert made up of all the kids on the holiday. They either do this with their particular bedroom crew, or sometimes just with friends. Dramas, songs, recitals and game shows are always there . . . the main purpose is to get the youth leader up on stage for some embarrassing quiz or guessing game that he has no chance of winning.

VARIETY KEEPS THE KIDS INTERESTED.

John and I often do a concert after this event, ending up with some kind of appeal, depending on the flow of the weekend. It's always successful to have a laugh and a challenge on the same night.

The sessions that we do, depend largely on the leaders. Sometimes they will have a theme in mind, and sometimes they will just tell us what kind of kids they are expecting on the weekend and let us decide on the subjects. Because of our ministry we can chop and change at a fair rate of knots and usually include all sorts of interaction and audience participation in the teaching.

I suppose, most of the time, people want us just to challenge the kids to take another step with their Christian lives or to sort out just where Jesus fits into their everyday situation.

Some youth leaders book a speaker just to 'speak' and they do all the trimmings themselves. Sometimes, of course, they actually do the lot! All the systems have their good parts, although I think that taking the kids away and keeping an eye on them is enough, without doing the teaching as well! So there we are: Physical, Mental and Spiritual.

ADAPT TO THE SITUATION.

John and I have been involved with these types of weekends for the past sixteen years, and as you can imagine, we've certainly seen some funny sights and experienced some weird situations! You see, all sorts of people go on youth weekends:

'We want our kids to go on with the Lord and take a step further with Him.' This is a general cry and normally we nod and get on with it; however, in this particular case, we arrived to a slightly different scene. Armed with lots of seminars and activities on 'Going on with God' and things like that, our suspicions were first aroused by the actual centre itself. For a start there was a lack of Christian-type posters around the place, no evidence of the usual 'Welcome to our Christian

Conference Centre'-type stuff at all. Strange . . . ah well, not to worry.

Then the brats arrived. They were carrying at least one ghetto-blaster each and they were all on. (Not that I particularly object to that – but normally the ground rules are that one person brings the music for everybody to listen to.) Then the personal tellys started to appear in the extremely noisy dorms, and it was like they'd moved in for good and had no intention of ever coming out again! It was at this point that a thought crossed our minds.

'I don't think these kids are Christians.'

Again, not that it mattered apart from the fact that we'd been asked to take these kids 'forward in the Lord'. A quick chat with the youth leaders revealed that the only contact these kids had with church, was that the youth club they went to was in the church hall. To be members of the youth club, you had to stay in for the dreaded 'God Slot', which, as you can imagine was flavour of the month for these street kids! So now, we had quite a few hurdles to leap over. These weekenders were fairly hostile to us from the word go but we thought that, by the time we'd done a session with them, they'd mellow.

Fat chance! Halfway through the first session, I was ready to go home. They sat with sullen faces all the way through. They wouldn't even look at us! We managed to get a small response by the end of the hour but nothing like it should have been. So it was time to take the youth leaders to task. You know, we couldn't believe it when they cheerfully said to us, 'Oh, they're always like that with the speakers. They hate that part of the weekend, but they know that if they want to come away with us, they have to come to the sessions or be sent home.'

Terrific!

KEEP IN TOUCH WITH KIDS' NEEDS.

We had a lot to sort out that weekend, mainly because the leaders hadn't worked out what was best for the kids. Oh yes, they knew what they wanted to happen, but it wasn't at all where the kids were at. *It's desperately important to take your young people into account when putting on these things.* Be real, work out what they can cope with – and for goodness' sake tell the speaker!

In the end, we gave the kids a pep talk. We told them that we were not going to hold Bibles over their heads all weekend and that it was fine by us if they had no belief in God at all. (This raised a few eyebrows!) We'd been booked to do our stuff and they were at liberty to disagree and challenge us as much as they wanted. 'At the moment,' we added, 'we are as bored with you as you are with us!' This seemed to go down rather well and we all had a great time from then onwards. *Once they knew that no-one was going to make them listen, they listened.* (This is a typical Brat reaction! . . .)

DEALING WITH MORE ESTABLISHED KIDS

OK. The more general youth weekend consists of fifty or more kids who do go to church, and have some kind of grounding on what Christianity is all about. They are excited because they are going away, and they'll put up with the Christian teaching bit . . . in fact, some of them will even enjoy it! They often bring loads of instruments and provide the worship time before the sessions. This is great, because most of them will have never played together before in their lives, and you get what amounts to a massive jam session every morning! It goes without saying that the chances of everyone being in tune is a non-starter, but who cares? We've got a load of young teens here *without the usual pressures of getting it right,* having a whale of a time and praising the Lord into the bargain!

Because of the vast selection of things to do on these holidays, you tend to find that *everyone excels at something.* The quietest people will get to grips with writing a script for some daft play for 'the dorm concert', others will shine in *noisier* ways. The pressure is off, no-one is looking at you with an ulterior motive and you really can feel the freedom of it all in the atmosphere. And it's in this atmosphere that *something very special happens*.

THE FRUIT FROM YOUR LABOURS

Something that has annoyed youth workers for generations! Yes! Brats start giving their lives to the Lord and sorting themselves out at a rate that would make your head spin!

Why is this so annoying? You see, all year (and years!) these hard-working leaders have been explaining the Gospel message, underlining the importance of a personal relationship with Jesus, laying down guidelines for an exciting Christian life and then WHAM! – one youth weekend and everyone becomes 'Super Christian'!

It hardly seems fair after all the work you've put into those kids' lives, that some bloke comes in and talks to your kids and they all react like they've never heard it before!

Well, John and I would like to encourage you about this situation; cut this bit out and nail it to your forehead:

Your groundwork with the young teens in your group has been a most valuable asset. Without your grinding through endless meetings, fun times and activities, these kids would never be in a position to receive Jesus, like they are now. Everything you have ever said to them regarding Jesus dying for them, the forgiveness of their sins and eternal life, has finally slotted into place. The penny has dropped . . . but you put the penny there in the first place. Reaping is easy . . . sowing is hard. Well done, you good and faithful servant!!

We've taken such a variety of these holidays, from totally disruptive kids to ones who come with their homework! In fact, the homework thing isn't that unusual.

Sometimes 'revising' has actually been on the timetable, and even that works well! I suppose it's all to do with sorting out what the kids you're taking away are like. *Some are very keen on written work* and will spend hours working out 'dingbats' and other word puzzles, whereas *others respond to activities*. We worked with a group of young people once, where we couldn't quite figure out what they liked doing. They seemed a bit shy of our microphones when we entertained them with quizzes and the like, and didn't like singing very much either. In the end we asked the youth leaders what made their young people tick and they said that the only thing they really liked was drama! This seemed strange as they were such a reticent crowd.

THE 'ARTY' TYPES

'Just give them a subject for each dorm, and they'll happily go away and work on it for hours,' they suggested.

By now, we were willing to give anything a go, so we gave them situations off the top of our heads. One of the stories was this – a man goes into a petrol station and when he goes to pay for his petrol, the garage attendant says he can have it for nothing. So naturally, the man goes back out and fills his tank right up. Then some ladies go into a supermarket and the manager tells them they can take a trolley and fill it with as much as they like, and it won't cost them a penny. These scenes and others like them could be expanded on, and then the last scene was someone just saying: 'God offers people eternal life as a free gift, and they leave it on the shelf.'

Well, by the evening, these dramas had turned into major productions, with everyone rushing around finding props and clothes and bits of scenery. The end results were just great . . . and the nice thing was that *quite a few of these kids realized (through their own dramas), what salvation was all about*. They had virtually written their own challenge and responded to their own appeal! *Sometimes, we just don't give our young people enough credit, do we?*

'I'd like to bring this chapter right up to date by telling you something that was said to us this week.

We were playing in some schools and working with the youth group in a church. On the last night, we played instead of the Sunday Service and a lady came up to talk to us.

She said 'I know this might sound strange, but I'd like to thank you for giving my daughters back to me.'

Yes, it did sound strange.

'You see,' she went on, 'when they were around thirteen years old, they saw you at a weekend away and they came back completely changed. They had been tottering on the brink of leaving the church and I was so worried about them, but when they returned from the holiday, they were just so different. And now they are older and still here, enjoying being Christians and involved in the church.'

Well, you can't get a better recommendation than that for a youth weekend, can you??

SUMMARY

Kids open up away from their normal environment and routine.
Mix fun with the spiritual – try not to separate them.
Involve kids in the programme as much as possible.
Be flexible, and adapt as needs arise.
Plan the weekend to suit the kids' needs and talents.
Remember that all your hard work throughout the year will be rewarded.

CHAPTER SIXTEEN

School

WHEN we ask kids if they will be happy to leave school, the surprising majority say 'No.' Although everyone pulls school down – it's almost a tradition – a bit like school dinners really, it's tradition to loathe school dinners, but if you've been inside a school lately you'll know that school dinners are normally very good. The choice is marvellous, catering for vegetarians, plus a great selection of things like curry and lasagne. Kids will always complain and say that it tastes like dog food . . . but they still eat it. Obviously they feel the same about school in general. *They hate going there – but they don't want to leave.* All their friends are there, their security is there.

When I was at school I wasn't a Christian and so I have no personal feelings to go on, only the experience of talking to thousands of kids who are Christians at school. *One of the main worries is that they feel they are not doing enough to stand up for their faith.* Indeed just the other week when we brought this subject up at a conference with 300 schoolkids, there were tears of exasperation as they tried to explain how *guilty they felt about not witnessing every moment of the day.*

BE CAREFUL NOT TO ADD TO THEIR PRESSURES.

Please take this in. *Your kids are desperate to tell their friends about Jesus* . . . this is highly commendable, but before you give them your wealth of experience on the subject, *just have a quick check on your own life.* Are you frustrated to tears about your workmates?? Are you all wound up because you don't seem to have enough opportunities to tell your office about Jesus? I would suspect the answer is probably 'No', if you're honest. Now, I wonder why that is? Could it possibly be because we don't get the same kind of pressure thrown at us, as we put on our younger kids?

It seems to me, that to get *that* wound up means that someone has been reading these kids the riot act for not 'doing their duty' and getting out there and witnessing. I wonder if we quite realize what we are doing? You see, *it's so easy to point the finger* and tell some little thirteen-year-old brat that the Lord expects him to be a light in a dark world . . . but when was the last time you did it yourself?

And think on this . . . some kids get terribly upset when they watch the news, or see a film about the result of a nuclear war. They have nightmares for weeks and dread going out in case the world blows up while they are away from their family. It is a *real pressure on them, they are frightened, their imaginations are so much more alive* and they can see it all vividly in glorious Technicolor. AIDS is another reality, divorce yet another . . . believe me, *a lot of teenagers live in fear and dread of these things*. And then we come along and tell them that they are letting the side down by not talking to their friends about their faith. We tell them that God *expects* this of them, and they are the only ones in the world not doing it right. Then the nightmares start again . . . the punishment . . . the pressure . . . we are not good enough . . . we might as well give up . . .

BE AN ENCOURAGER.

Our young teens need encouragement and lots of it. There is so much negative teaching around. *Why do we major on the negative??* The occult, no sex, rock music is bad for you, you've not had your prayers answered because of some sin in your life!! It's the last thing our kids need . . . they need to be *shown what to do not what not to do!* We are so good at telling them what's wrong – but not so versatile when it comes to explaining the right way.

So, somehow, we need to start encouraging our kids,

cheering them on and not making them feel like the world's greatest failures.

They acknowledge much more readily than us that they are not doing such a wonderful job at school. Well, that's what they think anyway, but quite honestly, anyone who worries about their testimony at school is probably doing a terrific job. So how can we help them?

HOW TO BE POSITIVE

First of all, we can put their minds at rest. We can let them know that giving your testimony is not one of the Ten Commandments, that they are not going to lose their Christianity over it. God is not expecting them to go into school every day thinking, 'How can I get my faith into the conversation today?' *To actually feel like that is very destructive.* More hassles have been caused by people thinking that they *must, absolutely must*, give their testimony to someone every day, than I dare to think about. I know a lady who cannot let a day go by without telling someone that Jesus loves them . . . Well, that's all highly commendable, but with her it's almost a habit, an obsession. So if she gets to the afternoon without having told anyone, then she starts walking past people saying 'Jesus loves you' as they pass by. This kind of behaviour has earned her all sorts of nicknames and she is generally thought of as 'a bit weird'. No-one is walking around thinking 'Gosh, that woman must be a wonderful Christian, I think I'll become one too!' *To witness for Jesus must come naturally. It's not something you have to do* like reporting an accident or telling someone their flies are undone. When a good opportunity comes your way, take advantage of it, use it, but make sure you *wait for the right moment*!

THE RIGHT MOMENT

OK. Back to school. If there is an event taking place for young people in your church, *make sure you take plenty of photos*. It's easy for a kid to take some stupid photos of her and her friends getting thrown into a river on a youth weekend, to school to show her schoolfriends. Then when they ask where this took place, she can explain that she went with the youth club from her local church. Bingo! You are in! 'What church is that? I didn't know you went to church! How many went to the weekend? Were there any decent boys there?' That's the cue to get out more photos of the decent-looking blokes and explain a little bit more about the church youth group. *Now there's no need to try and explain the Gospel at this point.* She just tells them what a great time she had, and waits patiently for another opportunity later on. How hard can that be? So dish those photos out and let the kids take them to school to show their friends. It's no problem talking about exciting things that have happened in your life.

Since I wrote that last page John and I have been away for a weekend with around thirty young teens. The boys outnumbered the girls by four to one, so it was an interesting time! Anyway, the subject of being a Christian at school came up and we were discussing what they could tell their friends about this particular holiday . . . and the Lord intervened! Well, when I say that . . . what really happened was that one of the boys got stuck inside a wardrobe! As usual in a case like this, one of the other lads sauntered past me and casually mentioned that his friend was stuck in the wardrobe in their dorm. I went dashing upstairs, and as I got nearer I could hear the sound of thumping and bashing and much laughter. He was indeed locked in the wardrobe. So, trying not to laugh too much myself, I said, 'OK, gang, I think it's time we let him out.' And that's when they explained that he really couldn't get out. Apparently, he'd gone in there himself for a laugh, and shut the door, and somehow it had jammed. We could hear him scratching at the door and he told us he was OK . . . but we ended up having to take the wardrobe to pieces to actually get him out. The kids were in their element! And, strangely enough, *they couldn't wait to tell their friends back at school!* They really didn't need any encouragement!

WHAT ABOUT CHRISTIAN UNIONS?

I suppose Christian Unions are another problem for so many kids. Why is it that none of the decent kids go to them? They seem to have such a bad reputation. We accept the fact that there certainly are some really ace ones around . . . but the majority are not. Maybe it's just as simple as that . . .

There is a type of kid who likes joining clubs and societies and he tends to be the one who wears a birdwatcher's outfit and covers himself in badges. (Being birdwatchers ourselves we don't apologize for that statement!!) But seriously, maybe the others are just not the club-joining type. Especially if the Christian Union meets after school . . . I mean you've got to be a definite type of person to like staying behind after school when you could be free!

So, to make a Christian Union attractive to other species, they have to be well-run and provocative. For instance, what does the general poster for your local C.U. look like? Normally it's hand-drawn (badly) and has very small writing on it. It's all right for the Computer Club, they have theirs done on the megaprinter . . . Well, maybe someone should ask if they would do one for the Christian Union too. You never know, they might even enjoy the challenge!

WHAT YOU CAN DO TO HELP

As a youth leader, *we would ask you to consider helping your local schools with their C.U.s.* It's a great help to them if someone from 'outside' comes in once a week with *new ideas and some silly games.* The C.U. needs to widen its scope. One youth worker was telling me the other day of the C.U. he runs, which includes a game called the 'M & M Game'. He shrugged his shoulders and said, 'I really don't understand why it's so popular, 'cause it's quite horrible.' (Ah well, there you have it!) It's a quiz game where you watch a video and then have to answer questions on what you saw. If you get the answer right, you are rewarded with the first 'M' which is a marshmallow. If you get a question wrong, then you get to eat both the 'M's . . . a marshmallow dipped in an 'M' of your choice . . . Mustard, Mint sauce, Marmite or Mayonnaise! Obviously, the quiz always includes a few impossibly difficult questions!

But, through this game, the Christian Union has attracted hundreds of kids, who gladly sit through a short drama sketch or another attractive way of bringing home the Gospel, to make sure that they are there when the M & M game takes place! When Nigel thought of this game, we're sure he wasn't thinking, 'Wow! I've found the answer!' . . . it just happened. *You have to experiment.*

Your teenagers *need to take their lead from somewhere, especially at school.* It might be that they come up with some great ideas, *but they're not quite experienced enough to push the whole thing through.* They need your help. Most schools are totally happy to let a youth worker come in and organize a *lunchtime event.* If you work full time with youth, then you should have more time to put together something during the week that could spark off the start of a successful Christian Union.

A bit of encouragement here . . . just recently the 'lunchtime event' organized by outsiders has become pretty popular. Maybe kids are getting more used to having things like the Radio One Roadshow coming to their town, and they see lunchtime shows in a different light. Whatever it is, it's just starting to work well amongst Christians and non-Christians alike. The Roadshow method is working well, a lot of the time it's taking over from where a normal 'concert'-type situation would appear. The main value of this is that *you don't have to be able to sing or play an instrument to attract the attention of the local schoolkids.*

THE LUNCHTIME ROADSHOW

Maybe there's a bit of mileage in running through the basics here:

1. You will need three or four people to run it.
2. Although it's not absolutely necessary, it's good to have some kind of P.A. system and a few mikes.
3. Some taped music.
4. Lots of silly ideas for games and competitions . . . see chapter fourteen on 'Ideas for Action'.

Give your show a name (like the M & M game we told you about) and if possible have a backdrop or posters so that kids can identify you with it. Put the show on in the middle of the lunch hour – e.g. if lunch is 12.00–1.00 aim for a half-hour show running from 12.20–12.50. This gives the pupils time to eat their lunch and time to get ready for lessons either side. You might also find that the school has staggered lunch hours, in which case don't be put off if the kids are coming and going throughout your performance – it will be the only way they can attend.

Use some *decent taped 'chart' music* to bring the kids into the hall in the first place and then when you have enough to start the ball rolling, start yelling out for some volunteers. There's always a few loudmouths around who will push their friends forward! Once they have been up on the stage and played 'Chubby Bunnies' or something, then you will find you have drawn a crowd. From there you can introduce yourself and

121

explain that you will be coming in to their school once a week/month/term and have been invited there by the Christian Union (hopefully it will have a better name than that!). Ask for some more volunteers or maybe go down in the audience and have a chat with some of them . . . ask them what they think of their school. (Don't worry if they swear . . . *you* are the Christian not *them*!) Find out a few names and then try another game or competition. If you have access to a video, then some kind of quiz involving film clips etc., would be good. Don't worry if everything doesn't get a good reaction, just cut the duff things short and go on to the next thing. Just *make sure they get to know your name, the fact that you are with the C.U.* and if you are going to include some kind of application of the Gospel, *keep it short* and make sure that you are not *evangelistic*, you must not step over the line in school.

It is probably best to stick to a short drama sketch or amusing story to bring over your Christian stance. Lunchtime is a good time to start to *get to know kids*, and, as you are going to come back on a regular basis, there is no panic about getting the whole school 'saved' by the end of the hour!

After your roadshow, *stick around and talk to the pupils* . . . ask them if they enjoyed it and what they liked or disliked. They will soon tell you, and no doubt suggest things to add to the next one. There's nothing nicer than kids racing up and saying, 'Can I do that game next time?' or 'Can we have Mr Bean next time?' They will soon let you know whether it's worked or not!

The main thing is that you *give it a shot*. Maybe you've never done anything like this, but as an adult you have the edge on the kids when it comes to time and experience to organize events. *If you do a good job you will find that everyone in the school will appreciate your efforts*, from the pupils to the teachers and even the caretaker (if you clean up afterwards!!).

Roadshows are on the increase, so get in there first before your spot is taken by someone promoting blood transfusions or whatever!

SUMMARY

Avoid adding to the pressure kids are already under.

Major on the positive.

Being naturally like Jesus is the best example.

If you help your kids to get excited about Jesus and your church activities they will talk about it.

Putting input into school life via C.U.s can affect hundreds of kids and the staff at schools.

Mix in and get to know your community.

CHAPTER SEVENTEEN

Mission Impossible?

JOHN and I have been involved in over 500 youth missions up and down the country and feel well able to advise you on the pitfalls and successes that such an event can bring!

We've done missions for small villages where the local school only houses a few hundred kids and they all get bussed in from other little villages . . . which generally means that unless they have very kind parents to bring them in to a Christian mission . . . you are liable to find yourself with an audience of thirty or forty kids, for a week's labour!

On the other hand, we have been involved with city-wide missions that are so large that it's taken over an hour just to reach the school we were playing in, from the place we were staying in! And they have been almost too successful, with an overflow of hundreds of schoolkids who couldn't get in to the main event!

You must understand from the start that organizing a school's week or a youth mission *is liable to be a most successful situation.*

YOUR EXPECTATIONS

Recently, we were in a smallish school for a week and the area itself was pretty rough. We decided to explain to the local committee that we couldn't see more than around a hundred of the non-Christian kids coming to our main concert. They stared at us and then nodded dumbly, and we thought we'd burst their bubble. At the end of the week, we had around 130 schoolkids attend our final mission concert and we were satisfied that we had done our best.

The organizers, however, were still wandering around looking slightly dazed and eventually they came and confessed:

'When you first said that you expected a hundred kids to come to our mission we were so stunned that we didn't say anything. You see, we would have been over the moon to have seen twenty arrive . . . and quite honestly we thought that you had well overestimated, judging by the type of kid you'd been working with. So when you mentioned a hundred, we couldn't believe what you were saying!'

So, it's good to sit down and *talk about your expectations first*!

YOUR MOTIVES

Now, let's have a gradual look at all the things that go to make a successful event.

Why?

Yes, why do you want to have a youth mission in the first place? Believe me, people have them for the weirdest reasons. A common one is *'conscience'*. Yep, lots of people feel that it's time they did something for the 'young people in their town' and maybe they've read a book or been to a conference and heard the terrible statistics about young teens. Well, sorry, *that's not really a very good reason to have a mission*. As we've said before, kids are not daft, they *know when they are being conned* – so don't bother.

On the other hand, if this idea has come from your minister, maybe, and handed down to you as a youth leader, then grasp it with both hands while it's being offered! If you have a *heart for the kids in your area*, then grasp any opportunity to reach out to them. There's a lot more to the question of Why, but we'll come back to it later.

ONE THING AT A TIME

Who?
Yet another question that needs answering before we can move on. Another mission we worked on recently had a lot of problems with this one. You see, there were quite a few people involved in the running of it, and they couldn't decide who needed us most – so that 'gave us' to everyone! The young people in the church *needed encouraging;* the young people in the schools *needed to hear the Word,* the church members needed to have us round their houses for 'cosy chats' so they didn't feel left out, and the youth leaders wanted a *weekend's training* out of it! This was a bad idea and we felt like we were being pulled in four different directions, which basically meant that nobody got the best out of us.

So decide exactly what your town needs most and then pool all your energies into it. It won't be that easy to make this kind of decision, but you are much better off going for one specific goal.

A DIVIDED YOUTH WORK

If your youth group is small and you want to see young people added to it, then *target the school where most of your youth group go.* That way, you will already have *contacts with the kids themselves.* You will nearly always find yourself with the ridiculous problem of mixing the new kids with the kids that already go to your church. This is a major headache for a lot of youth workers, as *kids get so cliquey* with each other. In the same mission where the hundred estate kids came, we had this problem. The organizers had planned to have two separate meetings a week . . . one for their regular kids and one for the 'new kids'. When we asked why, they said that they couldn't see them *mixing* and that none of their regular kids ever came to the youth club they put on, which was open to everyone.

Admittedly, I was a bit annoyed at this attitude and said, 'Well, they are gonna have to get used to it! These kids need each other and the Christian kids had better start learning to live with it.'

This was greeted with a round of applause and the suggestion that John and I should be the ones to break the news to the youth in question. So, before the night of the concert, we got the churched young people together and told them of their 'duties' for the follow-up meeting. 'I want four of you on refreshments over there, and two of you on the door as people come in. Now, has anyone got a ghetto-blaster or something? Right, bring it here on the night with some decent music, OK?' Looking around at these astonished kids I said, 'Right, now these guys from the estate are gonna need your help. *They won't know what to do* and if you don't go over and offer them a tray of Cokes, you might find that most of it will end up on the walls. It's only because *they are in a foreign environment*, OK?'

There was silence for a minute, and the organizers were standing back waiting for the reaction.

'It won't work,' said one kid finally. The organizers visibly sagged.

'And why's that?' I asked cheerfully.

'Because the youth leaders won't let us do it,' they replied.

There was more silence, followed by gasps of surprise from these poor blokes. It turned out that the youth leaders had somehow been giving out the feeling that the church kids were 'not allowed' at the youth club. The emphasis had been thrown so hard on 'we're trying to get new kids in' ... that the church kids thought they were not allowed to come!

Have a think ... *maybe you have given the same feeling out without realizing it*. These kids were only too happy to help ... it made them feel *important and wanted*, whereas before, 'Outreach' was a word only associated with 'Not You.' So we have to make sure we know *who* this mission is for! Stop thinking that your youth group is against having other kids muscling in on it. A crowd attracts a crowd, and once you've got your kids past the fifty mark, it will really take off!

GET THE WHOLE LEADERSHIP AND CHURCH BEHIND YOU.

Backing

A mission is *not something you should try to take on by yourself,* or even amongst just a few youth workers. *It really requires the backing of at least one whole church.*

Every year, we get letters from young people who have seen John and me at various places and have been inspired to ask us to come to their area. This is great, and we *always encourage them* to try and get it off the ground, but it's not going to work if the *only* person who wants the mission is a thirteen-year-old boy who saw us somewhere else!

We suggest that the boy goes to his youth leader with our information and, if successful, gets the leader to contact us. *Many a fabulous youth outreach has had its wheels set in motion by one young kid.* We always make sure that the rest of the church know on whose recommendation we came!

The best way to feel happy about your mission is to make sure that *plenty of people are behind you.* For this reason, we always recommend that at least one whole church takes it on. A lot of missions we are involved in encompass all the eager churches of one area . . . this is great, as long as you can work together in some kind of harmony.

CHOOSING A VENUE

When we work in schools, we highly recommend that the main concert/outreach event is staged at *one of the school halls. This cuts out any arguments about whose church has the better hall, etc.,* and, kids are far more likely to attend something on *familiar ground* (like their school hall) than your church.

It's a funny thing, church. We have a lot of difficulty with Christians who are convinced that every kid knows where their church is. They say, 'It's the big one in town, you know, you walk past it to get to the bus stop.' Well, let me tell you now . . . *they have never seen it*! I know it might sound ridiculous to you that hundreds of schoolkids pass your church and don't know it's there . . . but they don't . . . honest! You see, it's not part of their world.

Ask a bloke in the street to direct you somewhere and chances are he will say, 'Well, go past The Three Feathers, till you get to The Royal Oak, now there's a garage on the corner by the A5 sign . . .'

The same directions from a mum would go like this: 'Turn left at the library and go past the infants' school and it's near Safeways.'

A Christian? . . . yes, you've guessed it . . .'Straight past the Methodist hall and cross over at St John's.'

A schoolkid . . . 'Down past the chip shop, turn round at the video hire place and there's a leisure centre over the road.'

I'm sure you can hear what we are saying!

Anyway, you need the backing of one or more churches and you need them to understand your motives for putting on this mission. Where you can get a team from several churches to work together, you can really work wonders for the youth in your area.

AIMING FOR MANY OR JUST A FEW

Schools

This is where every kid is. Fat, thin, ugly, handsome, rich or poor . . . they all have to go to school. *This makes school the most successful place to start* your event. If you reach out 'on the streets' you are only going to end up talking to the same dozen kids all week – fine if that's what you are after, but please don't get into the rut that a lot of people seem to fall into, and that's the egotistical 'We are after the street kids, man!' type stuff. We have watched Christians go into a town and supposedly give out invites to all the teenagers . . . whereas, in fact, they are only interested in talking to the few who 'look weird and could be into drugs'. Listen! . . . *Most kids are ordinary and don't do drugs*, they come from ordinary homes and watch ordinary things on the telly. They buy ordinary clothes from Top Shop and sit around in McDonalds. OK? And there are hundreds of them and they need Jesus just as much as your token Goth! *Get real*, and start mixing with the masses! All right, sermon over.

HOW TO APPROACH YOUR LOCAL SCHOOL

Right! Schools. The secret of a good schools mission is to go straight to the top. I know you probably have connections with Christian teachers – but it saves a lot of hassles if you go straight to the head teacher. You see, the thing is, your Christian teacher probably has enough to deal with without having to put her head on the block for you, whereas the Head will have an unbiased view. It won't matter if the Head is an out and out atheist, if he thinks that the programme you are offering is *educational and attractive*, then the bias is put aside in favour of the kids getting a lot of enjoyment whilst learning about your faith.

In our experience, *the Christian teacher is put under a lot of pressure* to 'sell' you to other teachers who might think that she is 'getting at them'. It also means that you probably only end up taking a few R.E. lessons, whereas the Head can give you the hall, the assemblies and lunchtime events much more easily and without the 'suspicious circumstances' radiated by the poor Christian teacher! Make sure you *check the dates* of your mission with the schools before you finalize anything, because the last thing you want is to find that your mission clashes with half-term or the school play (which means you can't have the hall!) The next thing you have to work out is whether you are going to run this whole thing by yourself, or whether you need *outside help*. Then, of course, there's the *timetable*, the *publicity*, the *itinerary*, the *follow-up* . . . Tell you what – let's split this into two chapters!

SUMMARY

Look at your motives and goals before anything else.
Go for one major thing at a time.
Get the youth group involved and mixing with new kids straight away.
Get widespread support from the Church in general.
You need their prayers and possible financial support.
Use neutral venues for your event.
Aim for the masses.
Seek to approach the heads of schools yourself.

CHAPTER EIGHTEEN

Bringing in the Professionals

IF you are not used to doing outreach on this scale, it will probably do you good to bring in someone who is. There is a small army of people who do schools work and youth missions as a full-time job. Organizations such as Youth For Christ, Oasis and Scripture Union would be able to put you in touch with able-bodied evangelists! (Of course, you can always use us!)

WHICH APPROACH IS BEST?

First of all, *you need to decide what kind of role you want your visitor to play*. If you have had an influx of musicians lately, then it would be good to use a theatre group or stand-up comic/speaker. If you haven't had music lately, then I would strongly advise you to use it. *Music breaks down barriers with young people* quicker than anything else I know. Of course, it has to be professional and something appealing to teenagers.

John and I set up a thousand watt P.A. system in a school hall and stay there all day. Just one song in an assembly can set the scene for the hundreds of kids you are likely to see during the course of the week. This one song, if well received by both pupils and teachers, will pave the way for you to take more lessons than you ever thought possible! If the kids like it, then the teachers will acknowledge it and begin to ask if they can bring their classes in to hear you again.

Take time to sort out who to invite. Phone around and *talk to the artists*, find out how *they* feel about your mission and what they *specifically* do. Then, when you have found your perfect guest, invite them down for a Sunday to talk over the finer details, and to meet the church. John and I enjoy meeting with the church before the event, because *it helps to inspire them to pray.* It's hard to explain something like this to your congregation, but is far easier if your *artists come and introduce themselves.*

TEAM WORK

Hopefully by now you will have a *small team of youth workers* committed to putting this whole week together, so now is a good time to find out the *needs and specific details* of your guests. You will need to *give your team detailed jobs to do*, so make sure you know exactly *who is good at doing what*. This is no time to be bashful . . . *if you are a good artist – say so!* It saves a lot of heartache when the posters are naff and you could have done better! If you think you are a suitable candidate to go into the schools and *liaise with the Head teachers*, say so. If *follow-up* is your thing . . . get in there!

Publicity
Once you know the Where and When, you can begin to get going on *letting people know what's happening*. Posters are all very exciting, but your biggest publicity will come from putting a *leaflet* into the hand of every kid at school. There is no point in doing this before the event. (Although the *posters* help the build-up beforehand.) The leaflet needs to be given out by who ever is taking the lessons/concerts at the school, at the time of the lesson. Kids then *take a leaflet if they are interested*, and not because they have been left on every chair . . . which is a recipe for paper aeroplanes and a bad reputation with the caretaker.

In our own missions, we favour making sure that schoolkids

get something out of the deal . . . and so if you are charging for the main event, make sure that schoolkids get in cheaper. The easiest way to do this is to give out special invites with *'Half price with this voucher!'* splashed across it. Be careful to give them just to *schoolkids* and not to adults. This will ensure that most of the kids that come to the main event will not be Christians and will also be there first – so if you run out of room, at least it's only the Christians that didn't get in!!

It's good to use any publicity available, so *tell your local papers and the local radio what you are planning to do*. We have had loads of interested media wanting *interviews and photos* for local interest. Your *local paper loves anything to do with schools*, because if they can come in and take a picture of you performing in the hall with loads of kids . . . it means that every kid in the photo is going to buy the paper! The *same with local radio*. They might want just an interview with you, or perhaps they will come into the school and interview the kids on their reaction to having you in their lessons. Once again, it just adds to the number of listeners to their programme.

Timetable

Please make sure you check with your guest on the amount of work he *expects to do*. Normally, John and I split the day into three parts – morning, afternoon and evening – and will work for any two of them. *Trying to flog your guest morning, noon and night will only result in him being too tired to do his job properly*. If you expect him to teach in school all day . . . don't even think about giving him your youth group to 'mingle' with in the evening. *'Mingling' may not sound like work to you, but to him it will just be another session of answering everyone's questions*. Please try to be fair and you will get the best out of your guest!

Evangelism and Your Local School

Please be aware that *it is against the law to evangelize in school*!! This may come as a shock to some of you, but believe me it's true. Your only reason for being in the school is to *educate and stimulate the kid's minds.* This means you can go in to an R.E. lesson and explain what your faith means to you, but on no account can you apply that faith to the pupils. Students have to go to school by law, therefore they are not there 'of their own free will', so the only time you are free to do any out-and-out preaching, would be at the *concert at the end of the week*, where the kids are paying to come or are coming by invite, and are there of their own free will (going to school is compulsory!). This is then an 'out-of-school' situation and although you should still take it easy and not go at it like a 'bull at a gate', you can explain the Gospel to them.

You should keep in the back of your mind, that *whatever goes on at the evening event is bound to get back to the Head eventually* – and you want to be able to go back into that school on a further date!

If you are inviting a full-time worker to help you on your mission, he should be well aware of this situation . . . but it doesn't hurt to check it with him.

Accommodation

Again, going by experience, your guest will want to stay with a family or couple he can *relax with*. If it is at all possible, he should be able to *eat at this house too*. Many organizers love the idea of inviting the guest out to a different house each night for a meal, so that he can personally meet as many members of the local churches as possible – unfortunately, *this is not a good thing for your guest.* He has just spent all day being grilled by loads of kids, he's given his testimony umpteen times and would now like to go *back to his room, relax and then eat with people who already know where he's from* and how long he's been working with young people etc., etc. *It's very important to switch off* – and if you have been with him throughout a gruelling day at school, you will begin to understand what we mean!!

The Main Event

If everybody does their job, it can go like clockwork. Let's just go through the list . . .

1. Four people arrive an hour before it starts to set out the chairs and make sure the guests have everything they need (if they are musicians, they will already have been there around an hour getting set up).
2. A small team need to man the refreshments. A break is a good and necessary thing. It gives the team time to meet with the kids.
3. The counselling team need to arrive half an hour or so before the meeting starts. Make sure there's an area to use for talking to kids who want to know more about Jesus after the programme.
4. A handful of stewards are necessary to stand at strategic points around the building: a. The loos. b. Any open doors. c. Outside. Remember, you are not necessarily dealing with Christian kids who are going to come in and sit down.

Counselling

Most missions like to have some sort of appeal at the end of the programme. Have a dozen competent people ready to talk to kids. Teenagers will come out to talk for a variety of reasons, so check that your counsellors are aware of this and *make sure they ask them why they want to talk*. Some kids will come out because their friends did, some will not be up to making a commitment but will want to know more about Christianity, others might be ready to give their lives to Jesus. It's important that you understand what the teenager wants.

As we keep pressing on you . . . *take them seriously*, even if they've just come out with a friend and feel a bit giggly . . . it's still worth chatting to them and asking if they enjoyed the concert and if they understood the message.

Follow-up

If you are going to take names and addresses of any contacts, then you will need to *have something to invite them to afterwards*. There are a few pointers here that need to be taken on board . . . A lot of young people are taught not to give their name and address to strangers, so *don't press it*. They may, however, be happy to give you their name and form number, in which case the follow-up can be done by any Christians in the school. You need to have figured out beforehand exactly what form your follow-up is going to take. *It's good to have something special lined up* – a barbeque, some food and a video – something they will feel relaxed about coming to. If you can plan this beforehand, it means you can give your enquirers an invitation before they leave the concert. If this is not possible, then tell them you will be writing to them with news of another great event they might want to come to. Kids love receiving letters . . . so either way will work as long as you keep your promise.

Nurture Groups

Youth work is all about commitment, it is tough and there are no easy ways round it. If you want to see new young Christians grow in their faith, then I'm afraid it is going to cost you a lot of hard work. New Christians need looking after, and it is just no use pushing them off to the nearest church and hoping they will cope with the foreign atmosphere of the Sunday Service. They have to be nurtured, and this means starting a meeting especially for them. This is the point where a lot of youth leaders go off the idea of having a mission, because up till now they have been able to lean rather heavily on other people to help . . . but this is the bit that you really have to do yourself!

This kind of nurture group can be held at a house, or in a comfy room in your church. It needs to be for new Christians, people that are 'just looking' and also for some of your own churched young people (to add support and life for the new ones!). A totally unchurched kid needs to learn very simple things like: What is a Bible? What's it for? How do you pray to

137

someone you can't see? Tell me more about this Jesus character. It will all be very new to them and even the most obvious things to you, will be a mystery to them. That's why this group is necessary. Most of them wouldn't cope with church, they wouldn't understand it and they wouldn't stand a chance to grow. John and I both think that it's better not to introduce the church service to a new Christian for at least six months. Give them time . . . think how you feel about your service, and then put your feet in their shoes! Not nice, eh?

Nurture groups will be your biggest challenge. They are time-consuming and frustrating, but if you can get to grips with it, you won't lose those new kids. It's well worth the effort – but if you think you can't cope, then don't even begin to organize a youth mission until you can put your money where your mouth is . . . OK? The young people in your area are your responsibility, certainly people like John and myself can come and give a boost to what you are doing all the time, but at the end of the day we will be packing up our bags and moving on. The new kids will be left with you. Having said that, we don't shelve our responsibility and have bags of mail to prove it. Kids often write to us after an outreach and keep in touch for years. Sometimes whole classes write to us through their teachers, so some of the follow-up is ours and we hope to do it well . . . but the majority of the responsibility will be yours, so make sure you are ready for it! And if you are – go for it! The rewards are great!

SUMMARY

Choose the right approach for your event.
Find out how to get the best out of the artists/evange-
lists.
Get a good team round you.
Plan publicity, timetables, accommodation.
Stay within the law!
Counsellors need to find out what kids want.
Have a follow-up plan.
Hard work will reap its rewards.

CHAPTER NINETEEN

The Last Word

W E thought it would be nice to hand over the last chapter to the people who really matter. Yep, the kids! So, over the last year as we have been doing our rounds in schools all over Britain, we set a small survey going. We told the schoolkids that their answers would be featured in this book, so, as you can imagine, they went to town.

So here we have five popular questions, and some very astute answers . . . read, learn and inwardly digest!

WHAT'S YOUR ABSOLUTE FAVOURITE THING?

Believe it or not, the most popular answer was 'Chocolate!' We were quite surprised about that, although 'boys' and 'girls' came a fairly close second. In this day and age of 'eat your greens', kids still prefer 'stuffing my face' as one boy put it. Mind you, those of you who run a tuck shop will no doubt be able to second that!

Computers were also very popular as an answer. Youth leaders please take note and either get into it . . . or find a kid who is?

Another answer that came up time and time again was *'Watching teachers do something wrong'*. This is a wonderful moment in the history of school life and somehow *it makes you feel like it's okay to carve it up now and again*. I can remember our history teacher breezing into the class with his flies undone and his shirt poking through the gap ... it was glorious and caused no end of hilarity for our class. Strangely enough it was the notorious Kathy who finally went out to the front, took him to one side and whispered in his ear. A more grateful history teacher I've yet to meet!

Appearances, of course, are *always important* which is why one young girl wrote down her answer ... 'My cover-up to hide my spots (the little I have got.)' And David from Market Drayton wrote, 'My absolute favourite thing is abseiling down a 75ft cliff face.' I tend to think he doesn't do this every weekend, but it was certainly an impressive answer!

Another popular response was 'My room'. Ah yes, the day you get your own room and don't need to share it with anyone else is an absolute joy. It's almost a must when you become a teenager, there are *so many secrets* and heartaches and things to write down and posters to sigh over and fantasies to live. And how brilliant to stick one of those 'Keep Out! This is a Danger Zone' type notices on your door! And it also explains the reason a lot of the other answers were 'My absolute favourite thing is bashing up my brother!'

WHAT'S THE MOST BORING THING IN YOUR LIFE?'

Where to start? It's amazing how the word 'boring' conjures up *different things in kids' minds*. The outright winner, as I'm sure you will have guessed, was 'School'. Well, they do spend rather a lot of time there, don't they?

Hot on the heels of that answer came '*The News* and documentaries', or as one lad put it, 'the most boring thing in the world is pointless documentaries e.g. the life of the Brazilian Mongo tribe and how they affect the world. It really is what you need when you've finished your homework, isn't it??'

Documentaries, *The News* and *World in Action* all feature

heavily in this slot and can actually be made worse if you add the other most boring thing which is . . . black and white television, and black and white films. Yes, well, this is the age when if you even have a computer without a full colour screen you're underprivileged! . . .

I still find it fascinating that some kids, when they are small, actually think that the world used to be in black and white! They see old photos and old films and put two and two together . . . if *they* were in black and white, it stands to reason that the world was too. Obvious really, isn't it?

Another real humdinger of a bore for kids is 'gardening programmes', *Songs of Praise*, and 'elections and politics' . . . Maybe one day we'll get the Christian community so together that we'll be able to read: 'My most *favourite* thing is *Eastenders*, *Top of the Pops* and *Songs of Praise*!! . . . Ah well, one can only dream . . .

And here's a selection of the 'also rans':

The Most Boring Thing in the World is:

'Life.'

'Mr Chappell's assembly.'

'Having lectures off my mum.'

'Vegetables.'

'*Baywatch*.'

'Playing with my sister.'

'Sunday afternoons.'

'Homework.'

'Listening to opera.'

'Pollution and the idiots who create it.'

'My granddad's stories.'

'*Home and Away* and Kellogg's Pop Tarts.'

So now you know!!

AT THIS MOMENT, WHAT IS THE MOST IRRITATING THING IN YOUR LIFE?

By now, the kids are getting clever and the answers are getting smart. *'Keeping up my street cred . . . what a hassle for such a hip dude!'* Yes, we like that one!

Then we got 'The most irritating thing is *questionnaires!'*

Ooh! I've been stung!

People are also high on the list of irritating things. Top has to be *'brothers'*, they come up far more often than sisters! However, most kids specified a reason for their brothers and sisters being irritating:

'My sister, because she always nicks my socks and Body Shop shampoo.'

'My sister, because she takes my things without telling me.'

'My brother, because he always watches sport on the TV.'

'My brother . . . the monster.'

And there are a fair amount of other types of humans that they don't take to either:

'My mum.'

'My dad.'

'Parents.'

'This boy in my class called Alex.'

'Boys showing off.'

'My sister and parents treating me like a little kid.'

I am sure that you will have heard these complaints before, but *maybe you can use some of them as a basis for discussion*?

Then there are those other irritating factors that we would love to know the reasons behind! . . .

'At this moment? My hamster.'

'Making the coffee.'

'My bookcase because it always falls down and squashes my leg.'

'Getting a detention from a teacher for not doing my home-work and it isn't supposed to be in for a day.'

'Everything.'

I'll let you in to a little secret here . . . my most irritating thing as I'm typing this book . . . is hay fever!

WHAT DO YOU MOST LOOK FORWARD TO WHEN YOU LEAVE SCHOOL?

The most original answer, although naively written, was:

'My tea!'

It wasn't quite what we had in mind, but it was a cracking answer, wasn't it? Actually, it was quite sad to read that *most kids don't seem to have anything much to look forward to.* Some wrote that they would like a job and some wages, but most of them just *enjoyed the thought of all that 'freedom'.* When we sat and talked through this issue with older kids, the majority said that they were not looking forward to leaving school at all! At the end of the day they preferred to be *safe with people they knew and not go out to a strange new world.* It all keeps coming back to the fact that young people have so much more pressure now than ever before . . . they are taught that a job is very hard to find and *it makes them feel failures before they've even tried.* They read the papers and the story is the same, it is a no-win no-hope situation that they enter on leaving school – even with the right exams, etc. We've been into classes where they are taught how to go to an interview and how to write their CVs . . . but somehow the underlying feeling is that 'you can give it a try, but don't expect anything'. No wonder they don't want to leave. As a youth leader, it would be great if you could *encourage them in this situation in any way you can.*

A lot of kids were looking forward to driving a car, getting out of the rut and spending some money. Others? Well . . .

'Going round the world.'

'Doing what I want.'

'Having my own home.'

'Celebrating.'

'Going in the army.'

'A rest.'

'Going fishing all the time.'

'Freedom.'

'Being able to pig out in my own place.'

and . . .

'Ripping up my school books.'

Naughty but nice, eh?

We kept this next question till last, because a lot of the answers are pretty amusing and whether you like it or not you will identify with them! Ah, but have you said them to kids . . . or did someone say it to you when you were a kid?

WHAT IS THE MOST STUPID THING ADULTS SAY TO YOU?

It's very hard to know where to start with this one. Sometimes the pupils have given reasons for why they are such stupid comments but, like it or not, you've heard them all before.

'You're grounded.' . . . Not so much stupid as dead common. The words every kid despises, guaranteed to cause every possible mood and strop in the world. Does it work? Hmm . . .

'Tidy your room.' . . . But how are they ever going to find anything? It might be a mess, but everything's in its place!

'Calm down.' . . . When the girl you fancy has just gone off with your best friend and your hormones are turning somersaults . . . how are you supposed to do that? Young teenage years are the times when your emotions hit screaming point.

'I won't tell you again.' . . . But they do. Again and again, and does anyone ever listen?

'You were the one who had it last.' . . .Great, eh? These kind of comments make me laugh and drive kids round the bend. It seems like at fourteen every single thing you have ever touched disappears immediately afterwards! Spooky, eh?

'*No buts!*' . . . Because young people can be so inventive with their excuses, we often don't give them a chance to *actually explain* their side of the story. Maybe now and again it would be worth listening to the 'other version' before you say, 'Calm down, I won't tell you again!'!

'*What are you doing?*' . . . One kid had added in brackets – 'when they've been watching you for ages'. It's not always easy for a teenager to *understand the meaning behind a question like that*. Do you genuinely want to know because you are ignorant, are you trying to be *sarcastic* because you can't believe anyone could do that so badly, or maybe you know darn well and want to hear the kids own up to it?

Now here's a few we will run together:

'Act your age!'

'How *old* are you?'

'Hasn't he grown??'

'Oh grow up!'

'You're older now, you should know better!'

One kid had added to his answer . . . 'That *really* bugs me.'

At this age you are always going to be too young or too old. If you are misbehaving, then 'How old are you?' is going to be aimed at you, to show how childish you can be. On the other hand if you stroll out of your bedroom lathered in make-up with a skirt up to your neck, then 'How old are you? turns into 'And just how old do you think you are, Miss?'

Grow up . . . act your age . . . you're not old enough . . . you're too young . . . haven't you grown – confused or what??

We are not saying that these comments shouldn't be made, but more trying to show you how kids think and *how they sometimes misunderstand what's going on*.

Okay, here's the best of the rest:

'Turn that radio down!'

'When I was your age I didn't do that.'

'Sweet dreams.' . . . (Not sure why, but a lot of kids didn't like this. Maybe it's childish??)

'Homework!'

'We'll see.'

'Watch your weight, dear, you'll soon regret it when you're older.'

'Eat your vegetables.'

'Don't be cheeky!'

'School will be all right.'

'Who do you think you're talking to?'

'Behave!'

'Bed!'

'You should know better.'

'How was school today?' (Now come on, that really is a stupid question!)

'Just watch your attitude.'

'I think you've got some growing up to do.' (Well, yes, I'm thirteen!!)

And at the top of the list we have just a few more:

'If someone hits you, walk away.'

'If you fall out of that tree and break your legs, don't come running to me.'

'Eat all your meat on that chop!'

And Dave and Andrew both agreed that hitting your brother with a pillow or some other blunt instrument didn't deserve the comment:

'You'll have someone's eye out with that!'

And very top of the list was that terrible two-lettered word:

'NO!'

We have had a lot of fun chatting to young people about these topics and happily I can say that we have not been 'studying' them in any way . . . *just enjoying their company*. It would be very worthwhile you taking note of what they have to say and learning from it. Although many of their comments are naive, they are in their own way trying to get you to understand the ups and downs of their lives. And they are important: the friend not turning up, the colour of a sweatshirt, the haircut, the letter-writing, the row with someone in class . . . oh especially that . . .

Homelessness is on the increase, so is suicide amongst young people, so take time to understand, and to listen. Please, please . . . *go easy on the Brat Pack.*

SUMMARY

Getting it wrong is common to us all . . . show your humanity and laugh with them when you do get it wrong.

Stand with them as they try to get to grips with the adult world.

Be patient when emotions run high.

Enjoy being with your youth group.